city-lit

PARIS

Oxygen Books

Published by Oxygen Books 2009
Reprinted 2010

A CIP catalogue record for this book is available from the British Library.

ISBN 978–0–9559700–0–9

Typeset in Sabon by Bookcraft Limited, Stroud, Gloucestershire

Printed and bound in India by Imago

Praise for *city-lit PARIS*

'Brilliant … The best way to get under the skin of a city is to read a novel, a short story, a poem set slap bang in the heart of things. This literary guide to Paris, with the best of contemporary and classic writing about the most elegant city of them all, Paris, is the perfect read for travellers and book lovers of all ages. And a fabulous way to expand anyone's reading list!'

Kate Mosse, best-selling author of *Sepulchre*

'A great and eclectic set of writings and an original book on Paris.'

Sylvia Whitman, Shakespeare & Company, Paris

'It's terrific – all the best writing on this complex city in one place. We will be putting it on the reading list for our MA.'

Professor Andrew Hussey, author of *Paris: The Secret History*

'An essential guidebook to Paris without which you would be intellectually lost. It maps the Paris of the imagination.'

Kate Muir, best-selling author of *Left Bank*

'I really love the idea – when taking a trip, to have a book that offers just what you are offering … short pieces by good writers that capture the essence of a place.'

Orna Ross, author of *A Dance in Time*

'For readers who don't want to leave their minds at the airport.'

Celia Brayfield, novelist, journalist, and author of *Deep France*

Editor's Note

Paris: the most written about city in the world. There's enough good writing for at least six anthologies – which makes choosing difficult. But I hope readers will find plenty to fall in love with in our word-portrait of this most alluring and complex of cities.

The *city-lit* series aims to give you the most entertaining, lively, and fascinating writing about our greatest cities, bringing them to life … whether you visit them in person or from your armchair. As well as Paris, 2009 takes us to London, Dublin, Berlin and Amsterdam. We hope you'll follow us there.

For those with an eye for detail, I have followed the spelling and punctuation of the original texts, which are not always consistent with each other (e.g. some use a lower case 'r' for *rue*, some an upper case).

So, enjoy Paris!

Heather Reyes

Contents

Contents

Contents

Cities of the dead

Past tense

Living it up

A few words about Paris ...
from STEPHEN CLARKE

Paris is not entirely unique. You can sit in cafés, wear designer clothes and even have sex in lots of other towns.

It just *feels* unique, as if everything you do, from buying underwear to chewing a hunk of baguette, is somehow more stylish because you're doing it in Paris. Certainly Parisians act as if they're unique – not as a community but each individual one of them. It is the city of *moi*. As they walk down the street they're thinking, look at *moi*. Even when they're kissing a friend on the cheeks, they're saying it – *moi, moi*.

And the obsession driving each *moi* is its lifestyle. Parisians have elevated lifestyle to an art – no, more than an art, it is (as only the French can say properly) a *raison d'être*. In summer, they close off a whole chunk of the road running along the right bank of the Seine – the city's main throughway – to create *Paris Plages*, a chain of imported beaches, riverside cafés, performance spaces, even *pétanque* pitches. Block a main inner-city artery so that people can play *pétanque*? Not many capitals would do that.

Similarly, the new *Vélib* scheme – cheap bike rental – was instantly adopted by Parisians as a chance to glide about the city looking stylish, as well as being a great new chat-up opportunity. "*Bonjour*, you have rented a *Vélib*? So have I, what a coincidence. Destiny has obviously decided that we must sleep together."

Admittedly, this love of lifestyle does have its downside. As soon as the *Vélibs* were introduced, you saw impatient Parisians jostling around, trying to push in front of each other to get a bike. Because waiting is not part of their lifestyle. The person in front is preventing *moi* from being where *moi* really wants to be.

So when a chic Parisian office worker barged in front of me to get his *Vélib*, I knew that he wasn't just being bad-mannered. No, he had an urgent appointment with himself and his lifestyle. It was probably imperative for him to go and sit outside a café before shutting himself away in the office. If he waited for me to fiddle around selecting my bike, he'd miss the chance to watch that new

1

secretary walk past in her tight skirt. One of these mornings she is sure to notice him, and then who knows what will happen.

It is the city's addiction to the *moi*-first lifestyle that has attracted writers to Paris for so many centuries. The average writer is, after all, even more egocentric than a Parisian. What's more, Paris is the true home of the intellectual, a place where you can talk total arty-farty twaddle and, as long as you are passionate about it (and preferably squinting through a haze of cigarette smoke), people will actually take you seriously.

Fortunately, though, there have been plenty of brilliant writers either visiting Paris or living here, and the book you're now holding is full of anything but twaddle, except perhaps for the samples of my own writing.

And what strikes me about reading Balzac, Flaubert, Orwell or de Beauvoir on Paris is how little the city changes. Superficially, yes – Balzac's heroes didn't have to battle their way onto a metro during a travel strike – but deep down things are always the same. There are still foreigners getting mistreated in swanky kitchens exactly as George Orwell was. Even some of the streets in Hugo's *Notre-Dame de Paris* are almost unchanged, and the darker ones can certainly smell pretty medieval on a Sunday morning before the cleaners come round.

My own first visit to Paris was inspired by a book – Zola's *Le Ventre de Paris* (The Belly of Paris), a novel about the often unappetizing things that went on in the city's food market at Les Halles. Being too hard up to buy a decent guidebook, I marched off in search of the market using only the free Galeries Lafayette map they give you at the railway station, and was disappointed to discover that the glass-framed market halls had been knocked down and replaced by a hideous shopping mall about twenty years earlier.

However, as I wandered away, deep in literary mourning, I stumbled into the rue Montorgeuil and was confronted with bloody hunks of horsemeat, skinned rabbits, live lobsters and heaps of pungent mushrooms with the soil still clinging to their roots. A *boulangère* had set up a stall in front of her shop and was gleefully handling money and bread while sneezing into her palm with a disregard for hygiene that would have brought out the bacteria police back home. I was in Zola's novel.

These days, people moan that the area around the rue Montorgueil has gone posh – there is now, for example, a trendy Japanese restaurant that does mango sushi. *Merde alors.* But Zola would recognize the epicureanism of a street where every other business is dedicated to food. And you can still buy a baguette that has been fondled by a baker's dubious fingers. Mango sushi, OK, but polythene bags for baguettes? *Non merci!*

The area of Paris where I now live has many timeless qualities to it. It's the Butte aux Cailles. A picturesque name, I thought when I first moved in – Quail Hill. But no, a friend explained that quail was an old word for prostitute. Apparently the hill used to be a prime cruising zone. And in a modern way, it still is. There's a small gang of ladies who go round sticking massage ads on trees and lampposts. Hand-written, too. None of your new-fangled colour printing technology for these quails.

I often see people filling water bottles outside the Butte aux Cailles swimming pool. There is a spring beneath the hill, and a fountain where you can collect the water, free of charge. These days it is checked for purity, of course, but even so, it is a part of daily life that must go back hundreds of years.

Nearby is the small local bookshop, which advertises an in-house "public writer". No, not a resident author who will lecture you on the problems of the omniscient narrator – this is a person who writes your letters for you if you can't spell too well yourself. What century are we in again?

And the wonderful thing is that none of this is done for tourists or because the state or UNESCO has provided a grant to ensure that future generations will always be able to witness ancient French folk customs. It is simply unchanging, everyday Paris.

There is, however, one quaint folk custom that is state-subsidized. Every year, generally in winter, the French government workers go on strike, and the nearby Place d'Italie comes alive with balloons, revolutionary songs and the fragrant odour of *merguez* sausages being cremated on barbecues. The atmosphere is usually very festive, with old friends meeting up and comparing banners. Last year, I went and interviewed some of them for a French TV programme, and the protesters were in a hearty mood despite the rain. I met a group of strikers from a suburb of Paris who were sitting out a shower in a café.

"How many times have you been on strike?" I asked one man.

He had a think and replied, "this year?"

Next I found a chanting Parisian social-security worker and interrupted him to ask about his all-time favourite strike or protest march. He consulted his colleagues and they decided that "it was last year, when we went to Brussels." Yes, these demonstrations are such an integral part of their lifestyle that they even go on striking holidays.

So if you come to Paris hoping to visit some of the places mentioned in this book, and your trip is disrupted by a transport strike or protest marches, don't be disheartened. It's just one example of Paris imposing its lifestyle on you. All you can do is adopt the strategy I used with the *Vélib* queue-jumper – accept that *c'est la vie* and give a resigned Parisian shrug.

You don't know how it's done? It's very simple. You put on a facial expression that says "what do I care, we're all mere grains of sand in the infinite desert of the cosmos," you imagine that a pair of overweight parrots has settled on your shoulders, and then try to lift them six inches higher without tipping them off. Get practising before you visit Paris – it's a key exercise in all the city's yoga classes, so you'll have some catching up to do.

STEPHEN CLARKE is the author of a number of novels set in France, including *A Year in the Merde* and *Dial M for Merde,* as well as *Talk to the Snail*, a handbook for anyone wishing to get the best out of the French lifestyle. He lives in Paris.

"I love Paris ... "

The world is full of people who love Paris. If you know the city already, you'll be one of them. If you're about to go there for the first time, then you too will soon be part of the 'I love Paris' tribe – a tribe that is scattered all over the globe. Australia is about as far from Paris as you can get, but here's Australian Janelle McCulloch celebrating the city in La Vie Parisienne. *She loves Paris in all its seasons, but particularly as it moves into autumn.*

It's early autumn as I write this in my tiny apartment near the St-Sulpice church, and the season is settling comfortably over the Left Bank like a woollen scarf wrapped around the city's neck. Most people don't realise that Paris is more beautiful going into the colder months than at any other time. Under a dignified sky of Dior grey, you can see the 'bones' of the city, including its noble architecture, through the brittle branches of the trees. Somehow, the city seems finer, grander, more spectacular. The shimmering cognac shade of the Seine under the morning sun (which changes through the day to a luminous petrol blue and, finally, to a silver the colour of evening slippers at twilight), the grand grey of the famous cobblestone avenues and the fine oyster-shell grey of the buildings combine to give the city an almost gentlemanly feel. The city is distinguished, poised and more handsome than a Frenchman in a black tie.

This morning, as I walked out into the place St-Sulpice, where the morning light was still blinking in bleary reluctance over the buildings, you could smell the new season in the air. In the Luxembourg Gardens the park was being redressed for autumn with a light coat of copper leaves, while over in the organic market at boulevard Raspail, plump pumpkins and squashes were replacing strawberries, cherries and lavender on the open-air stalls. The rain, which had fallen lightly like pearl-grey tulle through the night, had stopped, although the streetlamps still shone like Carrier diamonds in the pale light. And everywhere you looked, there was a compelling beauty that made the 'oh' catch in your throat. The city was, in all its autumnal splendour, a romantic pastiche of poetic gestures, and it was perfect. Just perfect. The kind of day that makes you believe the ideal can be real.

I am not the only one who feels this strange and all-consuming seduction. All over Paris, people – even the Parisians themselves – are rediscovering and remembering how beautiful and sensual their city can be. Call it *dalliance français*, if you'll forgive the pun, but everyone's falling a little in love with Paris all over again.

Janelle McCulloch, *La Vie Parisienne*

❋ ❋ ❋

But it's not only foreigners who fall in love with 'The City of Light': here's a young Marie Darrieussecq, one of France's best-known contemporary writers – not born in Paris but humorously conveying a convert's enthusiasm.

I love Paris. It's the only city where I could possibly live. Because one of the great things about France is the centralisation: everything is in Paris. My husband is in Paris. My editor is in Paris. My thesis director is in Paris. My best friend is in Paris. My friends are in Paris. My house is in Paris. My cat is in Paris. My goldfish is in Paris. My bakery is in Paris. My email is in Paris.

My shrink is in Paris. And even my address is in Paris. In short, in Paris, everything is to hand. It's marvellously well organised.

In the beginning it was much more complicated: indeed, I was born a long way away from Paris, at the point where the frontier meets the ocean, tucked away in a corner. I had to study for a long time and take lots of trains, I even had to wait for the TGV Atlantique to be constructed, in short I had to wait until it occurred to someone to release me, before I could come to Paris. You can imagine how tired I was, how torn; I couldn't live, not without Paris. My house had been standing since the nineteenth century, my husband had been born twenty years previously, my cat's great-great-grandmother was already quivering with desire for the aforesaid's great-great-grandfather, my baker was vigorously kneading dough for baguettes I wouldn't be eating, and my shrink hadn't yet met me, which he greatly regretted. As for my best friend, constantly by my side, she was impatient to get on: she had the same problem as me. We were born in the same place, in that little corner a long way from Paris. Our lives were becoming increasingly complex.

Fortunately everything fell into place and turned out for the best. I live in the only city where I could possibly live. There are magnificent parks and gardens, as many cinemas as you could want, museums, shops, smart avenues, colourful neighbourhoods, and Parisians everywhere. I often walk around underneath the Tour Eiffel, between its four great arms. I head right for the middle, I look up and fall into the big hole that is the centre of the world. There are Japanese who come here for this reason alone; but afterwards they have to go and get on a plane and go an awful long way away. When I think that all of this has been put here for me, provincial girl that I was, I tell myself that life is beautiful, that the world is extremely well put together and that everything in it functions to perfection.

Marie Darrieussecq, 'I Love Paris', translated by Nicholas Royle,
The Time Out Book of Paris Short Stories

❈ ❈ ❈

The love-cum-puzzled-frustration of an Anglo-Saxon in the Gallic capital is captured by Michael Sadler in An Englishman in Paris. *As often in a 'foreign' country, the toilet arrangements come in for some special attention.*

Take the 95 from the rue de Rennes and head towards the Opéra. The bus goes down the rue Bonaparte across the Pont de Carousel with the Musée d'Orsay on your left and the Pont des Arts and l'Institut, home of the Académie Française, on your right. It then enters the monumental archway of the Louvre. The bus now drives through what must be one of the world's most magnificent architectural treasures – the majestic three-sided Cour Napoléon, the Pei pyramid, the reflections of the ornate stonework in the marble black water of the pools, the long vista up the Champs Elysées towards the Arc de Triomphe. What is perhaps even more remarkable than the view is that nobody looks at it. In the bus a lady explains the bandage on her finger, a man reads *Le Monde*, two *lycéennes* giggle, others stare into nowhere.

How do they do it? This zen-like ability to be oblivious to beauty is the result of a long process of assimilation. It takes time, practice and concentration. And it is an essential component of the art of being Parisian.

Conscious of the fact that I am still at the Kodak Gold stage of my exploration of the city – my eyes refocus, zoom, compose and click every time I see something that takes my breath away – I decided to explore Paris with the precise aim of taking it for granted.

In the past weeks I have got pretty much used to the majestic Place des Vosges, the romantic Butte aux Cailles, the swish 16th, and Chinatown in the 13th. I have also managed to tame the Jardin du Luxembourg. The Luco, as I have learned to call it familiarly, is divided into different areas: the games area where old men play chess and eat sandwiches wrapped in aluminium foil packets; the solarium near the *orangerie*, where chic retired ladies expose their skin to holes in the ozone layer; the carousel area, excellent for eyeing up young mothers; the *bassin*, where children and the same young mothers play with toy yachts under the lubricious gaze of senators gazing down on them from the panelled splendour of their palace; and the Lolita area on the southern extremity near the Lycée Montaigne, full of *jeunes filles en fleurs*. Last Thursday I managed to walk across the Luco without looking at anything. I am making progress.

I was, however, being blasé about the Paris I knew. More dangerous, because it could take me by surprise and reveal that I am still a mere novice, was the Paris I didn't know. So I decided to give a chance a chance. I would get on the métro, get off at any old station and walk.

Yesterday I found myself in a little square not far from the rue Rossini. The late afternoon light was golden, there had been a shower and the birds were singing *bel canto* in the trees. I contemplated this Parisian scene with emotion. It was like a Sempé drawing – the square, the prams, the geometric beds of flowers, the statue of DEC..R..S – the plinth with the name was cracked but it looked strangely like Marguerite Duras wearing a wet wig – the hut of the *gardien du square*, the barrow of the leaf sweeper and ... the *sanisette* Decaux.

The *sanisette* Decaux is a newish protuberance in Parisian street architecture. Public loos in France have been famous since *Clochemerle* and the municipal battle over the ornate iron *vespasienne*, the archetypal French urinal which reveals the legs and the head but hides the essentials – the French, as all users of *routes nationales* in France know, have always been public pissers. They were named after the Roman emperor Vespasian not because he was incontinent but because he was the first to levy a tax on urinals. France has always been famous for its loos since the reported disappearance of several tourists over the years down the infamous *toilettes à la turque*, the foot-soaking, trouser-drenching crouchers which are the bane of the clean-living Anglo-Saxon.

The *sanisette* Decaux is a high-tech answer to the Turkish death-trap. It is reported to be a TGV. A *très grandiose vespasienne*. It is named after Mr Decaux who runs the company which provides free municipal architecture in exchange for advertising space.

The *sanisette* – which, let's face it, is a repulsive word, managing to combine the sanitary with a coy diminutive in *-ette* – looks like a cross between a money box and a tin of spam. It is ugly but it has always fascinated me. How do they open? What are they like inside? Chintz and leather armchairs? I am an intrepid explorer who refuses no challenge. To the weak-hearted among you, may my example be a lesson.

The square was almost empty at this time of the early evening. No one was watching. The moment was propitious. I put my penny in the slot. Loo and behold the machine, instead of rejecting the coins, hummed, swallowed the cash and obligingly opened its sliding door. It was a pushover. With trepidation I went inside. The door closed behind me.

I found myself in an orbital space station. One moment in the square Rossini, the next in Mir. In order to record the moment for posterity I sat on the loo and took out my camera, and narrowly missed being drenched by the automatic flusher. Beware. The Turkish syndrome lives on.

My photograph taken, I decided to curtail my visit – climbers have been known to spend only seconds on the summit of Everest. But I couldn't get out …

Michael Sadler, *An Englishman in Paris: L'éducation continentale*

❊ ❊ ❊

You've heard the saying 'Good Americans go to Paris when they die' – well, most of them don't wait till then. Here are two of them – T. E. Carhart and Adam Gopnik – wallowing in everything Parisian, from the changing seasons to a cardboard cut-out of a French policeman.

Summer set in early and the sidewalks in the *quartier* came alive after hours. In a city where few apartments are air-conditioned, the terraces of cafés and restaurants become the common refuge from a withering heat in the evening. The long light of June and July encouraged those gathered at the outdoor tables to linger well into the night, while swallows threaded the air with their shrill whistles. Before the August dispersion, everyone in the neighbourhood seemed to revel in the slower pace that the heat imposed.

[…] As summer turned into fall, the neighbourhood streets assumed the changes both big and small characteristic of Paris at this season. The cafés at the corners of the boulevards pulled in their aprons of outdoor tables, leaving only one or two rows for the stalwarts who took their coffee in the undying hope of a ray of light through the gray-blue clouds. Along the avenues the opposing rows of chestnut trees faded to a rusty brown and reluctantly gave up their leaves, their overarching green tunnels turned into long black nets of branches. The chestnuts littered the pavements in the evening, to be swept into the gutter's remorseless tide at the following break of day; in front of the elementary school the sidewalks showed only leaves and husks since the boys raced to collect the hard brown spheres, perfect for throwing , as soon as the bell rang in the late afternoon.

T. E. Carhart, *The Piano Shop on the Left Bank*

✳ ✳ ✳

I've wanted to live in Paris since I was eight. I had a lot of pictures of the place in my head and even a Parisian object, what I suppose I'd have to call an icon, in my bedroom. Sometime in the mid-sixties my mother, who has a flair for the odd, ready-made present, found – I suppose in an Air France office in Philadelphia – a life-size cardboard three-dimensional cutout of a Parisian policeman. He had on a blue uniform and red kepi and blue cape, and he wore a handlebar moustache and a smile. (The smile suggests how much Art, or at any rate Air France, improves on Life, or at any rate on Paris policemen.)

11

My younger brother and I called the policeman Pierre, and he kept watch over our room [...] My first images of Paris had come from the book adaptation of *The Red Balloon*, the wonderful Albert Lamorisse movie about a small boy in the Parisian neighbourhood of Menilmontant who gets a magic, slightly overeager balloon, which follows him everywhere and is at last destroyed by evil boys with rocks. Curiously, it was neither a cozy nor a charming landscape. The Parisian grown-ups all treated Pascal, the boy, with a severity bordering on outright cruelty. His mother tosses the balloon right out of the Haussmannian apartment; the bus conductor shakes his head and finger and refuses to allow the balloon on the tram; the principal of the school locks him in a shed for bringing the balloon to class. The only genuine pleasure I recall that he finds in this unsmiling and rainy universe is when he leaves the balloon outside a tempting-looking bakery and goes in to buy a cake. The insouciance with which he does it – cake as a right, not a pleasure – impressed me a lot. A scowling gray universe relieved by pastry: this was my first impression of Paris, and of them all, it was not the farthest from the truth.

Adam Gopnik, *Paris to the Moon*

✶ ✶ ✶

A flâneur *is someone who strolls about the city with no particular purpose other than looking at everything and enjoying it. One of the best strolling companions has to be American writer Edmund White (best known for* A Boy's Own Story*). His fascinating little book,* The Flâneur, *is like ambling around Paris with a well-informed but easy-going friend. Here he is comparing Paris and New York, then telling us about the famous café life and bookshops of St-Germain-des-Prés.*

And no wonder Paris, land of novelty and distraction, is the great city of the *flâneur* – that aimless stroller who loses himself in the crowd, who has no destination and goes wherever caprice or curiosity directs his or her steps. In New York the stroller can amble along from the Wall Street area up through SoHo, the East and West Village and Chelsea, but then he must hop a cab up to Amsterdam and Columbus on the Upper West Side; the rest of the city is a desert.

In Paris virtually every district is beautiful, alluring and full of unsuspected delights, especially those that fan out around the Seine in the first through the eighth arrondissements. This is the classic Paris, defined by the Arc de Triomphe and the Eiffel Tower to the west and the Bastille and the Panthéon to the east. Everything within this magic parallelogram is worth visiting on foot, starting with the two river islands, the Île de la Cité and the Île St Louis, and working one's way up the Boulevard St Germain from the Île St Louis to the heart of St-Germain-des-Prés, with its trio of famous establishments, the Lipp restaurant and the twin cafés, the Flore and Les Deux Magots.

[...] The square has undoubtedly lost some of its intellectual lustre. Everyone is lamenting the boutiquification of St-Germain-des-Prés, and it's true that one of the best bookstores, Le Divan, has been replaced by Dior, that one of the few record stores in the area has been cannibalized by Cartier, and Le Drugstore – a late-night complex of tobacco stand, restaurant and chemist – has been supplanted by Armani. Louis Vuitton has installed a chic shop right next to Les Deux Magots.

OK, the move of Le Divan, which had been in the same place since its opening in 1921, to the outer Siberia of the *petit-bourgeois* fifteenth arrondissement really does spell a major loss to St-Germain-des-Prés and seriously compromises its intellectual pretensions. It was a bookshop (founded by Henri Martineau, a publisher who lived above the premises) where, incredibly, the staff were *friendly* and where the dusty window displays might be devoted to turn-of-the-century epigrammatic poets from Mauritius or to the previously unpublished madhouse rants of Antonin Artaud, dashed off after a particularly vigorous electroshock session. No cookbooks or slimming manuals, nothing to help in planning that next vacation or home improvement. Nothing but difficult literature and austere volumes of theory and philosophy. Fortunately, a very similar and even larger bookstore, La Hune, is just around the corner and usually open to midnight.

Edmund White, *The Flâneur*

* * *

Americans are not the only non-English English-speakers to discover the delights of Paris life. In recent years young Australians have been among the most enthusiastic adopters of the city (see Janelle McCulloch's piece that begins this section) – though Sydney-girl Sarah Turnbull found herself on a steep learning curve after accepting an invitation to visit Paris from Frédéric, a Frenchman she met in Bucharest.

That trip to Paris was more than eight years ago now. And except for four months when I resumed my travels, I have been living here ever since.

It was a city and culture I was familiar with – at least that's what I thought back then. When I was a child my family had toured France in a tiny campervan and my eyes had popped at the chocolates and cheeses. At secondary school I studied French and saw a few films by Truffaut and Resnais which had struck me as enigmatic and European, although I couldn't have said why. When I was sixteen we lived in England for a year and I came to Paris several times. In my mind, these experiences added up to knowledge of France and some understanding of its people. Then, a little over ten years later, my meeting with Frédéric drew me back, and when the time came to actually live in Paris, I figured belonging and integrating would take merely a matter of months.

Now, remembering my early naiveté draws a wry smile. The truth is, nearly all my preconceptions of France turned out to be false. It hardly needs to be said that living in a place is totally

different from visiting it. And yet this blatantly obvious statement does need to be said, particularly about Paris, the most
visited city in the world. A place I imagined to know after a few
nights in a closet-sized hotel room as a teenager and one summer
holiday with a Frenchman sipping *kir* on café terraces.

At times the learning curve has seemed almost vertical. The
social code I discovered in France wasn't just different from my
Australian one, it was diametrically opposed to it. For a long
time, I couldn't fathom the French and, to be fair, they couldn't
fathom me either. My clothes, my smile – even how much I
drank – set me apart. During my first year, dinner parties turned
into tearful trials. There was I, a confident twenty-eight-year-old
with the confidence knocked out of me, spending cheese courses
locked in somebody's loo, mascara streaming down my cheeks.

It hasn't all been tears and trials, of course. The truth is, if
France failed to live up to some of my expectations, in other
ways the reality has been far richer, a thousand times better
than my clichéd visions. [...]

If I had to pick one word to sum up my life in France, it'd have to
be 'adventure'. Every moment has been vivid, intensely felt. No doubt
many people who live in a foreign country would say the same thing.
But there is, I think, something that sets this country apart from many
other parts of the world. I know of no other place that is so fascinating
yet so frustrating, so aware of the world and its own place within it
but at the same time utterly insular. A country touched by nostalgia,
with a past so great – so marked by brilliance and achievement – that
French people today seem both enriched and burdened by it. France
is like a maddening, moody lover who inspires emotional highs and
lows. One minute it fills you with a rush of passion, the next you're
full of fury, itching to smack the mouth of some sneering shopkeeper
or smug civil servant. Yes, it's a love-hate relationship. But it's charged
with so much mystery, longing and that French speciality – *séduction*
– that we can't resist coming back for more.

Sarah Turnbull, *Almost French: a new life in Paris*

* * *

But perhaps we should allow the last word to the French themselves. After all, Paris is their city, even if it doesn't seem so at the height of the tourist invasions. Raymond Queneau (1903–1976) gives us some Parisians who clearly adore their city – though it seems they can't tell the difference between the Panthéon and the Gare de Lyon and speak a French that is less than pure Parisian. During a taxi ride, they try to interest Zazie, an impish, foul-mouthed provincial child, in the beauties of the capital. (Louis Malle made a brilliant film of the book.) And as a contrast, there's an excerpt from 'Nightmare' – one of hundreds of short stories by Guy de Maupassant (1850–1893) – capturing the weird beauty of the city at night.

With a light but powerful hand, Gabriel shoves Zazie on to the back seat of the taks, then he installs himself by her side.

Zazie protests.

'You're squashing me,' she yells, mad with fury.

'Promising,' remarks Charles succinctly in a calm voice.

He starts up.

They drive for a bit, then Gabriel indicates the landscape with a magnificent gesture.

'Ah! Paris,' he utters, in an encouraging tone, 'what a beautiful city. Just look, eh, how beautiful it is.'

'Don't give a damn,' says Zazie, 'what *I* wanted was to go on the metro.'

'The metro!' bawls Gabriel, 'the metro!! well there it is!!!'

And he points to something in the air.

Zazie frowns. Shezon her guard.

'The metro?' she repeats. 'The metro,' she adds scornfully, 'it's underground, the metro. Well Ida know.'

'That one,' says Gabriel, 'is the elevated.'

'Well then, it's not the metro.'

'I'll ksplain,' says Gabriel. 'Sometimes it comes out of the ground and then later rere-enters it.'

'Tripe.'

Gabriel feels helpless (gesture), then, wishing to change the subject, he points out something else they happen to be passing.

'How about that!' he roars, 'look!! the Panthéon!!!'

'The things you hear,' says Charles without turning round.

He was driving slowly so the child could see the sights and improve her mind into the bargain.

'Maybe it isn't the Panthéon?' asks Gabriel.

There's something crafty about his question.

'No,' says Charles forcefully. 'No, no and no, it isn't the Panthéon.'

'Well what would it be then in your opinion?'

The craftiness of his tone becomes almost insulting to his interlocutor who, moreover, hastens to admit defeat.

'I really don't know,' says Charles.

'There. You see.'

'But it isn't the Panthéon.'

The thing is that Charles is pig-headed, as well.

'We'll ask a passer-by,' suggests Gabriel.

'Passers-by!' retorts Charles, 'they're all bleeding clots.'

'That's true enough,' says Zazie serenely.

Gabriel doesn't insist. He discovers a new subject to enthuse about.

'And that, he exclaims, 'that's ... '

But he's cut short by a eurequation from his brother-in-law.

'I've got it,' roars the latter. 'The thing we've just seen, twasn't the Panthéon, course it wasn't, it was the Gare de Lyon.'

'Maybe,' says Gabriel casually, 'but it's past history now, let's not talk about it any more, whereas that, Zazie, just have a look at that and see if it isn't a lovely lump of architecture, it's the Invalides ... '

'You're talking through the back of your head,' says Charles, 'that's got nothing to do with the Invalides.'

17

'Well,' says Gabriel, 'if it isn't the Invalides, tell us whatitiz.'

'I don't know exactly,' says Charles, 'but at the very most it's the Reuilly Barracks.'

'You two,' says Zazie indulgently, 'you're funny little creatures.'

'Zazie,' declares Gabriel, assuming a majestic air which he effortlessly selects from his repertoire, 'if you'd really like to see the Invalides and the genuine tomb of the real Napoleon, I'll take you there.'

'Napoleon my arse,' retorts Zazie. 'I'm not in the least interested in that old windbag with his silly bugger hat.'

'What *are* you interested in then?'

Zazie doesn't answer.

'Yes,' says Charles, with unexpected gentleness, 'what *are* you interested in?'

'The metro.'

Raymond Queneau, *Zazie in the metro*, translated by Barbara Wright

✻ ✻ ✻

On the boulevards the cafés blazed with light; people were laughing, going in and out, having a drink. I went into the theatre for a moment or two. Which theatre? I have no idea. It was so dazzling in there that I found it depressing, and came out again somewhat cast down by the violent shock of the lights on the gold of the balcony, and the artificial sparkle of the enormous crystal chandelier, the lights leading down to the pit, and that harsh, false glare. I reached the Champs-Élysées, where the café-concerts seemed to be burning like so many fires among the green leaves. The flecks of yellow light on the chestnut trees made them look painted; they looked like phosphorescent trees. And the electric globes, just like pale but brilliant moons, like moon eggs fallen out of the sky, like monstrous living pearls, made the dirty, ugly gas filaments and the strings of coloured glass pale beneath their mysterious, royal, mother-of-pearl brightness.

I stopped under the Arc de Triomphe to look at the avenue,

the long, wonderful starry avenue leading into Paris between its two rows of lights, and the stars! The stars in the sky; unknown stars flung out here there and everywhere into the vastness of space, drawing their crazy patterns that fill a man with dreams and wonderment.

I went into the Bois de Boulogne and stayed there a very long time. A peculiar trembling had seized hold of me, an unexpectedly powerful emotion, a mental exaltation bordering on madness.

I walked for a long time. And then I retraced my steps.

What time was it when I passed beneath the Arc de Triomphe once more? I don't know. The city was falling asleep and large black clouds were gradually spreading out across the sky.

For the first time I had the feeling that something novel and untoward was about to happen. It seemed to me that it was cold, that the air was getting denser, that the night, my beloved night, was weighing heavy upon my heart. The avenue was now deserted, except for two policemen walking along near the rank where the cabs were drawn up, and on the cobbles, only faintly lit by the dying gas lamps, a row of vegetable carts on their way to Les Halles. They were driving slowly, loaded with carrots, turnips, and cabbages. The drivers were asleep and invisible, the horses walked with an uneven tread, silently following the cart in front on the cobbles. As they passed under each pavement light, the carrots glowed red, the turnips white, and the cabbages green. And one after another, these carts, red as fire, white as silver, green as emerald, moved along the road. I followed them, then turned into the Rue Royale and came back along the boulevards. There was no one there, no lights in the cafés, just a few laggards hurrying home. I had never seen Paris so dead, so deserted. I took out my pocket watch. It was two o'clock.

Guy de Maupassant, 'The Nightmare',
translated by Helen Constantine, in *Paris Tales*

❋ ❋ ❋

Le Menu

The French are justly proud of their cuisine. They've long led the Western world in the art of turning dead animals and what sprouts from earth into gifts for the most delicate and appreciative of palates. So it isn't surprising that food features frequently in writings about Paris – everything from lengthy, high-society dinner parties in Proust to the enthusiasms of today's young visitors. The delicate artistry of the Parisian pâtis-sière; colourful markets where displaying vegetables approaches an art form; cheese-sellers with a profes-sorial knowledge of their products; the availability of cheap, good food in even the most modest cafés – such are the usual perceptions of food in the capital whose waiters (there are about 120,000 of them, apparently) are regarded as following a worthy profession. In her book Touché, *French broadcaster and journalist Agnès Catherine Poirier highlights the importance of independent shops and cafés to maintaining the high standards in food and the unique atmosphere of Paris.*

I spent my youth in the 12th arrondissement of Paris in the Nation district, a petty-bourgeois area, neither grand nor louche, just quiet. Take my arm; I will walk you down my old street. You know how we love food, don't you? Well, let's start our tour with, on the right, the pâtisserie where on Sundays my dad would sometimes get me a *mille-feuille*. I'd eat it later layer by layer in the most unorthodox manner.

At the *traiteur*, the delicatessen, just next to the pâtisserie, we would get a little *barquette* of *tarama* (taramasalata) and *céleri rémoulade* (celery in cream) as a Sunday treat. Next to the deli, a butcher, a luxury fruit and vegetable mini-market and a wine shop: too expensive, *on passe*. Another butcher. A few metres on, the fishmonger's, a particularly good address where a horde of apprentices rush about to serve the clients queuing chaotically on the pavement. Expensive too, but, hey, *ce n'est pas tous les jours dimanche!* (It isn't Sunday every day!)

Let's have a look across the street. There is yet another butcher, a *fromagerie*, a pâtisserie, a bakery, a café, a newsagent, a Chinese delicatessen, an ironmonger's where I used to buy models of fighter planes to glue together to emulate my big brother, another fruit and vegetable stall and another café. From here, going up the street from the fishmonger's, we pass a wine shop, a pharmacy, a bakery, a ladies' footwear shop and a locksmith's.

Now let's cross rue Marsoulan, past the church on our right. Fewer stores, modern buildings from the 1970s and 'only' a florist, a coffee-roasting shop whose pungent smells permeated my childhood, a stationer's, a butcher, an Italian deli, two hairdressers, a wine shop, a mechanic's, the post office and a junk shop. Opposite, a little supermarket – Franprix – a bank, a bakery, a photo lab, a corset-maker, a café, a video outlet, a very old-fashioned clothes shop, a *librairie* [bookshop], a bric-a-brac shop and a beauty *salon* for self-conscious dogs. And here, sandwiched between dogs and books, is *chez moi*.

Here is a typical Parisian street; I dare say a typical French street. Since 1972, six out of the forty-one shops have changed. The old-fashioned clothes shop used to sell wine, but that change happened before I was four. The bookshop used to be a haberdashery selling ribbons and fabric by the metre, and in place of the video shop used to be a 'health' shop selling strange seeds and esoteric guides on how to live in harmony with nature. The corset-maker is about to close down, the newsagent has treated itself to a brand new façade, and the pâtisserie at the top end has indulged in a new coat of *marron glacé* paint. In the thirty-odd years I have known this street, there have only been a few cosmetic changes and a slight gradual evolution in response to technological progress: the video is here for a short stay, fabric sold by the metre has gone, and the corset has died.

In 2006, out of these forty-one shops, you will find only one franchise: the supermarket, Franprix, a national chain. But you won't find a single subsidiary of an international chain: no Starbucks, no Zara, no McDonald's. Remember this ... and now let's cross the Channel.

Agnès Catherine Poirier, *TOUCHÉ: why Britain and France are so different and why they do things in opposite ways*

✳ ✳ ✳

Poirier isn't the only one to prefer what is on offer on the Gallic side of the Channel. American Adam Gopnik remembers the relief of a meal in Paris after two days of London food; Canadian Jeremy Mercer recalls the modest pleasures of the poverty-stricken finding good vegetables at one of the many excellent street markets as he accompanies the legendary George Whitman (of Shakespeare & Company) on a shopping trip; and singer Alex Kapranos celebrates food in Paris – along with the French custom of staring and being stared at on café terraces.

Most people who love Paris love it because the first time they came they ate something better than they had ever eaten before, and kept coming back to eat it again. My first night in Paris, twenty-five years ago, I ate dinner with my enormous family in a little corner brasserie somewhere down on the unfashionable fringes of the Sixteenth Arrondissement. We were on the cut-rate American academic version of the grand tour, and we had been in London for the previous two days, where we had eaten *steamed* hamburgers and fish-and-chips in which the batter seemed to be snubbing the fish inside it as if they had never been introduced. On that first night in Paris we arrived late on the train, checked into a cheap hotel, and went to eat (party of eight – no, party of nine, one of my sisters having brought along a boyfriend), without much hope, at the restaurant at the corner, called something like Le Bar-B-Que. The prix-fixe menu was fifteen francs, about three dollars then. I ordered a salad Niçoise, trout baked in foil, and a cassis sorbet. It was so much better than anything I had ever eaten that I nearly wept. (My mother, I am compelled at gunpoint to add, made food like that all the time too, but a mother's cooking is a current of life, not an episode of taste.) My feelings at Le Bar-B-Que were a bit like those of Stendhal, I think it was, the first time he went to a brothel: I knew that it could be done, but I didn't know there was a place on any corner where you could walk in, pay three dollars, and get it.

That first meal in Paris was for a long time one of the few completely reliable pleasures for an American in Europe. "It was the green beans," a hardened New Yorker recalled not long ago, remembering his first meal in Paris, back in the late forties. "The green beans were like nothing I had ever known," he went on. He sat suddenly bolt upright, his eyes alight with memory.

Adam Gopnik, *Paris to the Moon*

✽ ✽ ✽

The following day was market day, and I had the pleasure of accompanying George on his rounds. Every morning of the week, open-air markets operate in different parts of Paris, selling fruit, vegetables, fish, cheese, and most everything else considerably cheaper than at the grocery stores. While the most celebrated of these markets was at Bastille, there were less expensive and more unruly versions at Belleville, La Chapelle, and place d'Aligre. We at Shakespeare and Company were fortunate enough to have a small market just down the street at place Maubert.

Three times a week, George roved the stalls, haggling for an extra pound of zucchini, negotiating down the price of carrots when the stalls were about to close, asking for an extra onion to be slipped into his bag. The great secret was that once the market shut at the end of the morning, all the produce that wouldn't make it through another day was thrown into empty crates and left behind. With a minor amount of scavenging, one could find most anything, and there was an entire community who waited for the markets to close so they could begin their shopping. That day, along with the vegetables we'd purchased, we found half a bag of apples suitable for stewing, some barely bruised eggplants, and, nestled alone in the gutter, a blessed potato.

Jeremy Mercer, *Books, Baguettes and Bedbugs*

✣ ✣ ✣

'It is a convention left over from Christian times.' In perfect RP, the receptionist explains that everything is shut in Paris. Today is a Sunday. The hotel is at the foot of Montmartre, by Rue des Martyrs, one of the finest Parisian food streets which, when it is busy, stimulates every sense. Each end is sealed, and there is a throng of shoppers prodding the produce and arguing with the stallholders. There are a few interesting buildings. If you look up as you walk to the bottom of the street, there is a ramshackle, shed-like building made of corrugated tin. If you look through the dusty windows, you can make out the shadows of huge papier-maché heads. At the top of the hill, there is the magnificent boulangerie Armand le Montel. There is always an intimidating queue, but the rhubarb *tartes* are wonderful. In the sandstone around the door are letters etched in Roman script: *À la Renaissance – pains français & étrangers. Pains chauds pour diners, pâtisserie fine & assortie, commands pour la ville.* On the opposite side of the street is the Rose Bakery. It's supposed to be an

English tea room, but they get it wrong in a spectacularly successful French way. You can sit outside on aluminium chairs that look as if Philip Starck made them. The brunch and particularly the quiche are good. Best of all, you get to sit outside and stare and be stared at. I'm unashamedly nosey and love it. People are fascinating, and checking them out is expected in Paris. They stare right back. I check out the old woman with the worn-out flip-flops while forking a roasted parsnip. I stare at the newly engaged couple, rings glinting in the low sunlight. I scoop chickpeas into my mouth. A kid dressed head to foot in denim wobbling past on stabilizers. A shuffling man with disappointed eyebrows, his neck swallowing his tiny chin. A skater clattering by on his back wheels. All meet the gaze unfazed as I swallow my broccoli. The Versace woman at the next table drops petits-fours into the yapping mouth of a Snowy-from-*Tintin* lapdog. If you stare at someone in a street in Glasgow, it's an invitation for a fight. If you stare at someone in Paris, it's because you want to look at them.

Last time I was here, it was a Friday and spectacular. A cheeky *chien* trotted perkily down the middle of the *rue* with a baguette in his mouth. *Champignons*, wild like delicate orchids, tumbled from wooden boxes. Monsters of the deep with claws akimbo lay spread on ice. Hares hung from hooks over coils of sausage and chickens that were thick-boned from healthy life. *Fromageries* oozed their heady pungency. *Pâtisseries* seduced me with the sweet scent of *tartes*, a crumb of which could exhaust your tastebuds for a week. Today is Sunday. Rue des Martyrs is desolate.

At nightfall, the options are still bleak. Chez Jean, one of the greatest restaurants I've ever eaten at, is yards away on Rue Saint Lazare. It is shut. Of course. It is open for a total of twenty-three hours a week. Not weekends. I cross Pigalle under the glow of busty neon silhouettes, up the narrow, cobbled Rue Piemontes. There are a lot of corners. Each is occupied. The occupants look like they're dressed for the Occupation: veil, fishnets, fag and a clutch bag – heritage whores in a historical re-enactment. On Rue Aristide Bruant, La Taroudant II is bright like my grandparents' living room – homely and welcoming, but a bit more Moroccan. Everybody smokes. Between courses. During courses. It is run by a couple in their mid fifties. M. Taroudant has a clipped moustache and a silver teapot in his hand. He brings the spout to the lip of a cup and raises his arm, slicing an arc of mercury through the air. He is stoic with the confidence of a practised and understated showman. Mme. Taroudant brings me a Tagine d'agneau. The clay is black with splashes hardened by the unforgiving fire, the ghosts of a thousand meals. Prunes fall from the stone. *L'agneau* falls from the Y-shaped bone. I can't tell what kind of bone. I try to summon some knowledge of *agneau* anatomy, but give up. I don't care. It is magnificent. Thank God for the Parisians who are unaware of a convention left over from Christian times.

Alex Kapranos, *Sound Bites: eating on tour with Franz Ferdinand*

✳ ✳ ✳

Francophile and avant-garde Modernist writer Gertrude Stein (1874–1946) had something to say about most aspects of France – and Paris in particular – including French cooking. She even explains the origin of the ubiquitous French croissant. We can only assume she has checked her facts …

Cooking like everything else in France is logic and fashion.

The French are right when they claim that French cooking is an art and is part of their culture because it is based on latin Roman cooking and has been influenced by Italy and Spain. The crusades only brought them new material, it did not introduce into France the manner of cooking and very little was changed.

French cooking is traditional, they give up the past with difficulty in fact they never do give it up and when they have had reforms so called in the seventeenth century and in the nineteenth century, they only accepted it when it became really a fashion in Paris, but when they took something from the outside like the Polish baba brought by Stanislas Leczinski, the father-in-law of Louis XV or the Austrian croissant brought by Marie-Antoinette, they took it over completely so completely that it became French so completely French that no other nation questions it. By the way the Austrian croissant was hurriedly made at the siege of Vienna in 1683 by the Polish soldiers of Sobieski to replace the bread that was missing and they called it the crescent the emblem of the Turks whom they were fighting.

Catherine de Medici in the sixteenth century brought cooks with her and made desserts fashionable, complicated Italian desserts, before that there had been nothing sweet in France except fruits. It was in 1541 that at a ball she introduced these desserts into Paris.

During the time of Henry the Fourth they went back to simple foods as he called himself the king of Gonesse where the best bread in France was made.

The French though did have ideas that one is apt to think of as American and Oriental, roasted ducks with oranges, and stuffed turkeys with raspberries, they ate the turkeys young, and a salad with nuts and apples in the time of Louis XIV.

Cook books were best sellers in France through the seventeenth century and in the introduction to the Dons de Comus, 1739, it was said that "the modern kitchen is a kind of chemistry," so it is evident that cooking in France always was logic and fashion and tradition, which is French. [...]

The Revolution of course stopped cooking and under Napoleon who did not know what he was eating, he rarely expressed a preference but he asked his cook to give him some flat sausages, his cook disgusted prepared an elaborate dish of finely chopped ingredients, Napoleon ate it without knowing they were not sausages.

But at that moment to save French cooking, Antonin Careme began cooking and he is the creator of present French cooking, but of course much simplified now because then neither material nor work was of any importance. [...]

Under Louis-Napoleon the writers and poets became the appreciators and critics of cooking as well as the financiers and the court, so Dumas wrote a cook-book, and this went on until the siege of Paris by the Germans and there in the cellars they cooked as elaborately as they knew how to disguise the queer things they had to eat.

Gertrude Stein, *Paris France*

✳ ✳ ✳

If you are one of those who shy away from eating the traditionally French escargots *and* grenouilles *(which sounds better than snails and frogs) then do spare a thought for the Parisians of 1870. As Gertrude Stein says (above), during the Siege of Paris, towards the end of the Franco-Prussian War, their diet was, of necessity, even more unusual – recorded in the journal of famous man-about-town, Edmond de Goncourt.*

Saturday, 24 September

In the capital of fresh food and early vegetables, it is really ironic to come across Parisians consulting one another in front of the displays of tinned goods in the windows of delicatessen shops or cosmopolitan groceries. Finally they go in, and come out carrying tins of *Boiled Mutton*, *Boiled Beef*, etc., every possible and impossible variety of preserved meat and vegetable, things that nobody would ever have thought might one day become the food of the rich city of Paris.

Saturday, 1 October

Horse-meat is sneaking slyly into the diet of the people of Paris. The day before yesterday, Pélagie brought home a piece of fillet which, on account of its suspicious appearance, I did not eat. Today, at Peters' restaurant, I was served some roast beef that was watery, devoid of fat, and streaked with white sinews; and my painter's eye noticed that it was a dark red colour very different from the pinky red of beef. The waiter could give me only a feeble assurance that this horse was beef.

Saturday, 31 December

In the streets of Paris, death passes death, the undertaker's wagon drives past the hearse. Outside the Madeleine today I saw three coffins, each covered with a soldier's greatcoat with a wreath of immortelles on top.

Out of curiosity I went into Roos's, the English butcher's shop on the Boulevard Haussmann, where I saw all sorts of weird remains. On the wall, hung in a place of honour, was the skinned trunk of young Pollux, the elephant at the zoo; and in the midst of nameless meats and unusual horns, a boy was offering some camel's kidneys for sale.

The master-butcher was perorating to a group of women: 'It's forty francs a pound for the fillet and trunk ... Yes, forty francs ... You think that's dear? But I assure you I don't know how I'm going to make anything out of it. I was counting on three thousand pounds of meat and he has only yielded two thousand, three hundred ... The feet, you want to know the price of the feet? It's twenty francs ... For the other pieces, it ranges from eight francs to forty ... . But let me recommend the black pudding. As you know, the elephant's blood is the richest there is. His heart weighed twenty-five pounds ... And there's onions, ladies, in my black pudding.'

I fell back on a couple of larks which I carried off for my lunch tomorrow.

Edmond de Goncourt, *Pages from the Goncourt Journal*,
translated by Robert Baldick

* * *

As a happy contrast to such hard times, Janelle McCulloch begins La Vie Parisienne *with a delicious indulgence ...*

In my favourite Paris neighbourhood, the famously romantic sixth arrondissement on the grand Left Bank, there is a ravishing pastry shop called Ladurée. You may have already heard of it, since it has passed into the realms of cult destinations to visit when you're lingering in this city, mainly because it's part tea salon and part visual feast. Beloved by everyone from fashion models to fur-wearing aristocrats, this sophisticated patisserie has become famous for many things – most of them fabulously calorific – but the one thing it's most known for is its macaroon, a dainty almond biscuit that has been elevated to a seductive work of art. Flavoured with everything from lime and ginger to bitter chocolate and even java pepper (a very Parisian shade of grey), this tiny confection has become the Chanel of desserts in Paris, thanks to Ladurée's decision to release new collections each season, just as the fashion designers do with the *haute couture* shows.

I pause here on an almost weekly basis, drawn to the windows like Holly Golightly in *Breakfast at Tiffany's* – and there are curious similarities, with Ladurée's signature mint-green boxes becoming as coveted as Tiffany & Co's duck-egg blue ones among the fashion set. (In a quirky twist, Tiffany's signature colour was supposedly inspired by Marie Anotinette's favourite shade, Nattier blue, while the 'modern' Marie Antoinette of Sofia Coppola's stylised film was inspired by Ladurée's sugary pastel shades.) I love to come to this irresistible patisserie when I want to be reminded of how beautiful Paris can be – and how even a simple macaroon can become art. Paris is like that, you see. Even the confectionery is sexy.

When I've finished gazing at perfect pastries I'll wander through lively streetscapes to the rue de Buci street market near St-Germain-des-Prés, an atmosphere-laden neighbourhood on the Left Bank that fulfils just about every fantasy you ever had about being in Paris. Here, my favourite ruddy-faced butcher and fishmonger – culinary counsellors with knobbly hands but beautiful hearts – proffer tips on how to seduce a Frenchman with a plump goose from the Périgord, before deciding that a hearty homemade soup is probably less work, and more seductive anyway. If there's time I'll stop for a hot chocolate at one of my favourite Paris bistros – crowded, century-old cafés that have thankfully retained the aura of their classic past, with wooden tables dressed in white paper and mirrors reflecting chalky blackboards and couples about to kiss. Afterwards, if it's warm, I'll make my way through Hemingway's and F. Scott Fitzgerald's old neighbourhood near the St-Sulpice cathedral to the Luxembourg Gardens and its parterres of pistachio-green chairs for a stroll among the statuary and formal gravel paths. Or I'll join the flavour-obsessed food lovers – including Catherine Deneuve, Audrey Tatou, John Galliano, Carla Bruni and Gérard Depardieu – at the organic market on leafy boulevard Raspail, where stylish Parisians fill string bags and elegant baskets with enticing limes, bundles of fresh basil, heirloom tomatoes, sleek leeks and asparagus spears so slender they could be the Kate Moss of the vegetable garden.

At the end of the day, I'll wander home through the enchanting narrow streets, full of good humour and, quite often, a little homemade cider, courtesy of a flirtatious merchant. I will usually have bought some *roquette*, a baguette, a couple of robust tomatoes and a bottle of organic Bordeaux to wash it all down with. And I will feel, as I always do in this sublime city, extremely grateful – and extraordinarily content.

This is my life in Paris, my Parisian life – or *la vie Parisienne*, as the locals say. And it's what I'd always imagined it to be. An education in style, glamour, gastronomy and grace in a place where even the asparagus spears are exquisite.

Janelle McCulloch, *La Vie Parisienne*

✻ ✻ ✻

Paris may still be the richest city in Europe, but not everyone can afford to eat in good restaurants. Colette Rossant recalls the modest reality for the unrich young in post-war Paris – not

*so different from how it is today, though without the MacDon-
ald's option; Stephen Downes tackles another side of the reality;
and in the course of a crime story, Stella Duffy's protagonist
gets irritated by all the fuss Parisians make about food.*

Food was a problem. *Chambres de bonnes*, usually on the top
floor of a building, were rooms that were owned by the apartment
dwellers below. The maid was supposed to eat in the kitchen of
the tenant she worked for. Today, these *chambres de bonnes* have
been transformed into elegant studios. Having no kitchen, I had
to eat out three times a day. Breakfast was no problem –*café au
lait* and a *tartine* (a piece of baguette slathered with butter) was all
I needed. I had my lunch at a small bistro, most of the time a prix
fixe *steak pomme frites* and salad. Sometimes I took *le plat du jour*
(daily special), which might be a *suprême de volaille en meunière*
(strips of chicken sautéed in butter) or *boudin noir* (blood sausages)
with steamed potatoes. Dinner was more of a problem. If no one
had invited me to dinner, I stopped at a *charcuterie* (delicatessen)
and bought readymade dishes to eat at my desk. Often it would
only be a few slices of ham or cheese with a vegetable salad. I was
happy but lonely – I didn't have many friends. School was not
going to start until the end of September, and I tried to occupy
myself by reading all the new novelists that I knew I was going to
study in my comparative literature programme: Simone de Beauvoir, Marguerite Duras, Robbe-Grillet. I also read Shakespeare
and Hemingway, who were all the rage in Paris.

Colette Rossant, *Return to Paris: a memoir with recipes*

❉ ❉ ❉

Sorry to disabuse you of a popular notion, but most French
almost never eat croissants for breakfast. The Gauls I know eat
fresh air, washing it down with strong black coffee. They rarely
have time for anything else, time being the commodity in shortest
supply in Paris. The popular image of the French sitting down to
wicker baskets lined with red-checked gingham from which spill

freshly baked croissants is somewhat misleading, then. They eat wonderful Parisian pastries at weekends, when they have more time. So I can't really tell you who eats all those croissants – not to mention the other bakery items – in the windows of Paris's hundreds of *pâtisseries*. Perhaps tourists or newcomers to France. I like breakfast and I like croissants and especially *pains au chocolat* or *pains aux raisins* (sweet pastries filled with a slim cylinder of chocolate or plugged with raisins).

Monsieur Da Costa is in his poky office in the corridor. I ask if he knows any good pastry shops nearby. The one up on the corner is said to be good, he says. 'Who says?' I ask. Madame Da Costa, he says with a broad grin. Mind you, he adds, he's never tried anything from there … He doesn't eat breakfast.

I take a left and walk perhaps eighty metres. A tiny corner commerce, La Daube *pâtisserie* should be more about stews and wet dishes (being what *daubes*, the cooking pots and that which is ladled from them, are all about). But it's a tiny pastry outlet all right, with floor to ceiling glass shone to a starshine, its floor tiled in glazed terracotta. A limited range of pastries sit on steel racks in glass display cases.

I choose a croissant and a *pain aux raisins*. The latter are sometimes called *escargots*, because they swirl like a snail's shell. Studding the helix and its stiff pastry-cream are the dried grapes, which look – if you let your imagination run away a little – a bit like dead blowflies.

Stephen Downes, *Paris on a plate: a gastronomic diary*

✳ ✳ ✳

Paris is small. The centre of Paris I mean. Like every other city with a stage-set centre, there are all those very many suburbs, the ones Gigi never saw, where cars burn and mothers weep and it is not heaven accepting gratitude for little girls. It is not heaven I am thanking now. I continue my walking meditation, past innumerable Vietnamese restaurants, and countless small patisseries where *pain au chocolat* and croissants dry slowly on the plates of high glass counters, and bars serve beers to Antipodean travellers who really cannot believe this city and call home to tell loved ones readying for bed about the pleasures of a beer in a café at ten in the morning. The glass pyramid can wait, this is art, this is the life.

It is a life. Another one.

There are no secrets. This isn't that kind of story. Nothing to work out. I can explain everything, will explain everything. But not yet. There are things to do and it must be done in order and the thing is, the thing is, we always had lunch first. She and I. She said it was proper, correct. That French thing, their reverence for food, an attitude the rest of the world outwardly respects and secretly despises. It's just food for God's sake, why must they make such a fuss? The linen the glass the crockery the menu the waiters with their insistence on pouring and placing and setting and getting it all right. Pattern, form, nothing deviating, nothing turning away, nothing new. Like the groomed women and the elegant men and the clean, clipped lapdogs. Nothing to surprise. So perhaps more than reverence for just food, a reverence for reverence, reverence for form. Female form, polite form, good form, true to form. Formidable.

> Stella Duffy, 'Un bon repas doit commencer par la faim',
> in *Paris Noir: capital crime fiction*, edited by Maxim Jakubowski

❋ ❋ ❋

The French love of ceremony in connection with food is picked up by Stephen Clarke – in his best-selling novel, A Year in the Merde, *he notes their surprising penchant for fast food (should we take it with a little pinch of salt?), and also treats us to a trip to a local boulangerie to buy bread. Incidentally, a huge proportion of the bread eaten in Paris is still made by hand.*

In French, the word "self" means a self-service restaurant. Ironic, really – the ego as cheap cafeteria, when France sees itself as one huge gourmet restaurant.

It's a pretty apt description, though, because, contrary to what they'd like us to think, the French love fast food. They tell the world that they eat only foie gras and truffles, but a huge percentage of them spend their lunchtimes and weekends with their face in a hamburger.

This is because fast-food restaurants do things to food that the French love. Staff in uniform, repeating little set phrases, arranging your napkin just so on your tray. It all appeals to the French sense of ceremony. Like it or not, a trip to a fast-food place is a culinary event.

The French love of food events is so great that it sends them completely insane when they go to the boulangerie to buy bread. The boulangerie is the only place in the world where the French will stand patiently in line. No, not true – they do it in the queue to buy cigarettes at the tabac, but that's only out of fear of getting ripped to bits by someone on nicotine cold turkey.

A visit to my local boulangerie was a real event. There were usually three or four women serving, or rather jostling each other, behind the cramped counter. They would dash around putting together my order, then had to queue themselves to tell the one woman on the till, the owner, how much I owed. Whenever I bought a baguette, the person who served me, and the owner too, had the right to squeeze it in the middle, as if they were addicted to the cracking sound the crust made. If I bought a cake, I could expect to wait a full five minutes while it was lovingly gift-wrapped and decorated with a ribbon. Occasionally a floury baker would emerge to watch the proceedings, and be shooed away by his wife in case he got flour in the till. Amid the chaos, the queue shuffled respectfully forward, even though it often stretched for yards outside the shop. People seemed to respect the queuing system here simply because it was part of a food ritual.

Stephen Clarke, *A Year in the Merde*

* * *

The traditional Paris café isn't just a place for consuming food and drink: it's a whole way of life. A place to see and be seen; a place to linger for hours over a single coffee or cocktail; a place to read the papers; to exchange ideas, to talk politics. In The World of the Paris Café, *W. Scott Haine explores the central role of this 'institution' in the social and political life of the capital, while novelist Georges Perec's Monsieur Winckler is clearly one of those Parisians for whom a favourite neighbourhood café is the centre of daily life.*

The nineteenth-century cafés of Paris were much more than places to get drink and food. Explaining why Paris had become the social centre of the world, Ralph Waldo Emerson wrote that its "supreme merit is that it is the city of conversation and cafés." Visiting Paris in the early 1840s, the young Karl Marx attended meetings of artisans and noted that "smoking, eating, and drinking are no longer simply means of bringing people together. Society, association, entertainment which also has society as its aim, is sufficient for them; the brotherhood of man is no empty phrase but a reality, and the nobility of man shines forth upon us from their toil-worn bodies." Indeed, Marx's historic first meeting with Frederic Engels took place in a Paris café, the famous café de la Régence.

Parisians had similar sentiments about this informal institution in their city. At the café Procope, Jules Janin, the pre-eminent literary critic of the 1830s and 1840s, believed, "French *causerie* [small talk] has exhibited its most lively impatience, its most dangerous zeal; all its briefs, all its paradoxes, all its scandals, all its resistance, all its opposition." Victor Hugo depicted working-class café sociability in a remarkably similar fashion in *Les Misérables*: "The wine-shops of the Faubourg [Saint-] Antoine have a notoriety which is historic. In times of trouble their words are more intoxicating than their wine. A sort of prophetic spirit and an odour of the future circulates in them, swelling hearts and enlarging souls." The Paris café, in short, was one of the cauldrons of conversation and thought in this "capital of the nineteenth century."

W. Scott Haine, *The World of the Paris Café*

* * *

After that he only went out to have his meals at Riri's. He would come at about eleven in the morning. He would sit down at a little round table, between the counter and the terrace, and Madame Riri or one of her daughters would bring a big bowl of chocolate and two fine slices of bread and butter. That wasn't his breakfast but his lunch, it was his favourite food, the only thing he ate with real pleasure. Then he would read the papers, all the papers that Riri took – *The Auvergne Messenger*, *The Soft Drink Echo* – as well as those left by the morning's customers: *L'Aurore*, *Le Parisien Libéré*, or, less often, *Le Figaro*, *L'Humanité*, or *Libération*. He didn't skim through them but read them through conscientiously, line by line, without making any heartfelt or perspicacious or indignant comments, but in a calm and settled manner, without taking his eyes off the page, not noticing the midday cannon which filled the café with the hubbub of fruit machines and jukeboxes, glasses, plates, the noises of voices and of chairs being pushed back. At two o'clock, when the effervescence of lunch subsided and Madame Ririr went upstairs for a rest and the two girls did the washing-up in the tiny working quarters at the back of the café and Monsieur Riri drowsed over his accounts, Winckler was still there, in between the sports page and the used-car mart. Sometimes he stayed at his table all afternoon, but usually he went back up to his flat at around three o'clock and came down again at six: that was the great moment of his day, the time for his game of backgammon with Morellet. Both played heatedly, excitedly, breaking out into exclamations, swearwords, and tempers, which were not surprising in Morellet but seemed quite incomprehensible in Winckler – a man whose calmness verged on apathy, whose patience, sweetness, and resignation were imperturbable, whom no one had ever seen angry; such a man [...] was able to seize the board with both hands and send it flying, calling Morellet a cheat and unleashing a quarrel which the café's customers sometimes took ages to sort out. Usually, though, it all calmed down pretty quickly so that the game could begin again before they shared, in freshly made-up amity, the veal cutlet with pasta shells or the liver with creamed potatoes that Madame Riri cooked especially for them. But several times one or other went out slamming the door behind him, thus depriving himself of backgammon and dinner.

Georges Perec, *Life: A User's Manual*, translated by David Bellos

✳ ✳ ✳

Would French intellectual and artistic life have become so pre-eminent without the cafés of Paris? Here's Parisian Agnès Catherine Poirier wallowing in all that traditional café life meant to her when she was young.

'Do you remember the first time you ever set foot in a café?' asked my six-year-old nephew. 'I think I will always remember the moment I order my first espresso,' he continued solemnly. Strange as it sounds, no, I don't remember *la première fois*, but my nephew is right; I should remember, as it must be, in the French psyche, almost as important as the first time one falls in love.

I do remember, however, from a very early age, going to a café with my dad, who would stand, not sit, at the counter, knocking back his *p'tit noir* in record time, sometimes grabbing a boiled egg from the metal pyramidal rack and cracking the shell on the *zinc*. At the time, sitting in a café seemed reserved for people with time on their hands or lovers stealing moments together. Everything ordered and eaten at the counter was, and still is, much cheaper than anything served at a table.

Sitting in a café was a rarity. I remember vividly how, as a little girl, after occasional blood tests I had to endure early in the morning on an empty stomach, my *maman* would take me to a nearby café for a hot chocolate and a croissant to reward my bravery: total luxury. I felt like the Queen of Sheba.

I also remember how my eldest brother, a strikingly handsome intellectual and one of the three heroes of my life (along with my other brother and Gene Kelly), would leave home in the morning without breakfast. I was seven, he was twenty, and *Monsieur* would have his breakfast in a café: 'Make it a large black coffee with a pot of hot water on the side and a *tartine*, please.' He would read the newspaper, scribble down cryptic thoughts on his notepad and the café's paper napkins, and then leave to go about his day. My mother thought it was a waste of money, but I was fascinated; this had to be what life was all about. One day, I'd do just the same. For me, there was nothing more desirable and symbolic than having coffee and a *tartine* in a café every morning; an incredible privilege, a sign of independence, wealth and personal fulfilment, thus surely the climax of one's existence.

I remember going to cafés with my *lycée* friends at the age of fifteen. We would sit (such extravagance) but order only coffee, the cheapest beverage available. We stayed for hours, gossiping, debating and sometimes canoodling in the red leather booths. When I became a student on the Left Bank, I'd sometimes spend my daily lunch allowance of 35ff on either a matinée cinema ticket or a *grand café crème* and *Le Monde* in the expensive and historical St-Germain-des-Prés cafés. It was silly, vain maybe, for a time, absolutely irresistible. I loved the Balzar on rue des Ecoles, a small brasserie that hasn't changed since the 1930s and to which Sorbonne professors still go between lectures.

I used to go to Le Vieux Colombier, on the corner of rue de Rennes and rue Vieux Colombier, where again *le décor*, with undulating curves on its ceiling and jewel-like lighting, hasn't changed since the art deco years. I'd go regularly in the afternoon to revise between two *confs* [lectures], and one day, at the next table, I spotted Lauren Bacall. I froze, can't remember how long my *rêverie* lasted, but when I finally snapped out of it, my *café crème* was stone cold. It was 1994, she wore trousers like nobody had ever worn them before; so chic I could have died. I bumped into her a few more times in the same café and each time I was mesmerised, enchanted: Hollywood was kissing me on the lips.

I also ventured to Les Deux Magots, opposite St-Germain-des-Prés Church. I had to. I couldn't not go. I wanted to sit where Sartre and de Beauvoir had sat, and where the legendary New Wave actor Jean-Pierre Léaud had perched nervously in *La Maman et la Putain*, Jean Eustache's 1972 masterpiece. The first time I went was also the last. I remember sitting down, looking around and waiting eagerly. Waiting for something to happen: a bolt of lightning, love at first sight, I don't know, anything. Nothing happened. The place was filled with Texan tourists, not a single French soul. I felt really stupid. I never set foot in there again. A few years ago, I got a call from a film producer who wanted us to meet. He suggested we go to Les Deux Magots. A shiver ran down my spine. I made up an excuse: I was busy this week after all, I was sorry, I would call him again. But I never did. The world of cafés is fraught with danger; choose carefully, don't get it wrong or you might lose your good reputation. It's fragile, you know.

Agnès Catherine Poirier, *TOUCHÉ: WHY Britain and France are so different and why they do things in opposite ways*

✳ ✳ ✳

'Takeaway' coffees and fast-food outlets may be making a small dent in traditional café culture and economic changes may be making it harder for even some of the better-off Parisians – and tourists – to eat out at the best restaurants, but Paris is still regarded as the good food capital of the world. And French cuisine is a world in itself – as chef Michael Booth discovers when he takes his family off to Paris and enrols in the most famous cooking school of them all: Le Cordon Bleu. But it's a steep learning curve and even trying to buy good ingredients at a French market proves quite a challenge ...

Our local turned out to be the Wednesday and Saturday morning market on Avenue Président Wilson at the bottom of Avenue Marceau. Large supermarkets are banned from central Paris, which can be infuriating if you are in a hurry. But for me a good French market is Disneyland, the Louvre, a Caribbean beach and a bungee jump all wrapped up in one: pleasure, art, relaxation and stimulation. From the first stall, Lorenzo's, the best fish stall in Paris, its icy scree resplendent with writhing crabs, hillocks of crusty oysters and alien sea urchins; on past the bounteous fruit and vegetable stalls; the compelling viscera of the butchers' glass cabinets; acres of cheeses, flowers and breads; until I eventually emerged back into the daylight an hour later, the outside world was banished. I was transported. [...]

But a good French market can be overwhelming the first few times you visit. Why are there crowds at one vegetable stall, yet another is deserted? Which fish stall is the freshest, and can their fish really be this expensive? And what on earth is that grey, spongy stuff in the butcher's cabinet? Slowly, through experience and, later, the tutoring of experts, I began to learn a few of the tricks of a successful trip. The first rule I figured out for myself early on, which was, to get the best service, to get the personal recommendations about which pâté to taste or what cheese is in season, or the odd bunch of complimentary parsley (or on one occasion a whole, ghostly white calf's foot), I had to patronise no more than a handful of stallholders – one from each category of fish, fowl, meat, veg, fruit and dairy, plus the Lebanese stall that sold a terrific sharp, fresh white bean salsa. (I soon learned never to buy bread from the market as it was not as fresh as at the *boulanger*'s). It was no good skipping from one stall to another picking up a head of broccoli here, a punnet of straw-berries there, as if in the opening titles of a Mary Tyler Moore sitcom. If you want to be treated with any respect you need to demonstrate your loyalty to specific stall-holders, dropping ten or twenty euros every week with the same people.

A good place to start was Jöel Thiebault's vegetable stall, also reputedly the best in Paris, where they sell ancient varieties of carrots in various, non-orange colours; gnarled, chunky tomatoes as big as grapefruit; rainbow-coloured turnips; and purple broccoli. Thiebault's family has sold vegetables grown on their farm in Carrières-sur-Seine here since 1873 and its staff, each of whom has the looks of a movie star, have perfected the art of ignoring customers, confident that Theibault's vegetables are so renowned – he is named on the menus of many of the restaurants he supplies – that they will endure an eternity to buy them.

It took time for the stallholders to get to know me. In fact, it was about a month before they acknowledged my existence at all and several times I petulantly walked away from stalls that ignored me (spiting only myself – French stallholders, like the shopkeepers, aren't overly troubled by mundane rituals of commerce such as the exchange of money). The first few times I attempted to buy something I would stand in line; be ignored as regulars were dealt with before me; until, finally, the stallholder allowed me to catch his eye for a moment. [...]

But gradually I perceived a change. At my fruit stall, when I chose a melon and passed it to the stallholder, he asked me when I planned to eat it. 'The weekend,' I replied. He sniffed the melon, squeezed it, shook his head and swapped it for another. I knew that, likewise, there were degrees of ripeness for Camembert, but I was still taken aback by the cheese woman's careful selection of one 'for next week'. She must have inspected about half a dozen before deciding on the optimum example, not just squeezing them, but kneading them with the serious intent of a reflexologist probing for a wonky metatarsal. The acceptance of the Président Wilson stallholders, signalled by a smile, or even a jokey admonishment when I walked past without buying something, felt like a personal endorsement of my shopping discernment.

Michael Booth, *Sacré Cordon Bleu*

✳   ✳   ✳

42

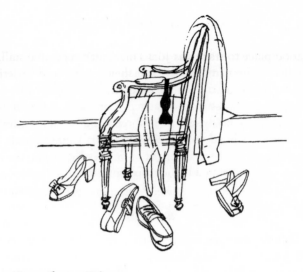

Sex in the City

The Folies-Bergère, the Moulin Rouge, Pigalle, the rue St-Denis ... the very name of Paris has for long been associated with the risqué and the just plain sexy. From the cheerful titillation of the can-can to the darker side of prostitution, writers have recorded this side of the city's personality. First, a little innocent fun as Colette's spirited creation, Claudine, celebrates a minor sexual victory soon after moving to the capital.

Well, after all, it's not so terrible going out alone in Paris. I brought back some very interesting observations from my little walk: (1) it's much warmer in Montigny; (2) your nose is all black inside when you get home; (3) people stare at you if you stand still in front of a newspaper kiosk; (4) people also stare at you when you don't let yourself be disrespectfully treated on the pavement.

Let me narrate the incident that gave rise to observation (4). A very good-looking gentleman followed me in the Rue des Saints-Pères. During the first quarter of an hour, inner jubilation of Claudine. Followed by a very good-looking gentleman, just like in Albert Guillaume's pictures! Second quarter of an hour ... the gentleman's step came closer; I hastened mine, but he kept his distance. Third quarter of an hour; the gentleman passed me, pinching my behind with a detached expression. A leap in the air from Claudine who raised her umbrella and brought it down on the gentleman's head with typical Fresnois vigour. Gentleman's hat in the gutter, immense delight of passers-by, disappearance of Claudine, overwhelmed by her too sensational success.

Colette, *Claudine in Paris*, translated by Antonia White

❊ ❊ ❊

Slightly less innocent than Claudine's brush with sex is the visit of the famous Danish writer Hans Christian Andersen to a Paris brothel at the age of 62. Having listened, over dinner, to the sexual exploits of the Danish journalist Robert Watt, Andersen is somewhat 'roused', as this diary entry records.

Sunday May 5th, 1867

Arrived at half past two in Paris, at the station in rue St Lazare and had lunch at three. At Café de la Recange met Watt who told me about his latest adventures with women. Wonder whether they are true. He's youthful and full of energy but not so polished that the kind of women he talks about would want to throw themselves at him. After I had dinner, I walked up and down full of desire. Suddenly I found myself in the kind of shop where they sell human beings: one was plastered with make-up, another plain and the third a real lady. I spoke to her, paid 12 francs and left not having sinned physically, but mentally without doubt. She asked me to come back and said that I seemed very innocent for a man. Many would find me contemptible. Am I in this respect? Wandered along the boulevard in the evening and saw in the cafés painted women playing cards and drinking beer and Chartreuse.

Hans Christian Andersen, *Diary*, translated by Mikka Haugaard

❊ ❊ ❊

When Paul West, in Stephen Clark's novel A Year in
the Merde, *sets up a date with a woman he hopes
to end up in bed with, he chooses a location straight
from the charming, romantic French film* Amélie *in
the hope that it might help his 'project' ...*

At my request we arranged to meet in Montmartre in the 18th,
at the place where Amélie Poulain's boyfriend looks down at
her through the telescope.

I took the ultra-modern funicular – a vertical metro – up to
the off-white, wedding-cake Sacré Coeur. I was five minutes
late, but luckily Alexa was over 15 minutes late, as most
Parisian women are.

We said hello with a chaste kiss on each cheek. She was brimming with understated sexuality in a battered old leather jacket,
a baggy-necked sweater and jeans with a hole in the knee. A fine-
looking knee, too. She had a camera slung over her shoulder.

I was brimming with under-used sexuality, and although it
was a bit blowy up here on Paris's mountain-top, I'd left my
shirt open enough to expose a manly hint of what I hoped was
photogenic chest hair. I don't have much, but what I do have
she was getting a good view of.

"Great to see you again," I told her.

"Yes," she agreed, apparently examining me for light sensitivity.

We then turned our backs to the Peruvian nose-flute band
that was currently entertaining the hordes of tourists taking
photos of each other, and looked out over Paris's rooftops.

In Van Gogh's day, Montmartre was a hill in the countryside
where artists came for inspiration, fresh air and cheap booze.
Now it had been well and truly sucked into the city, but it
still felt somehow outside, mainly because of the altitude. You
could look down over a chaotic jumble of grey zinc roofs that
had probably changed little in a century. With the Eiffel Tower
hidden away to our right by a stand of gold-leafed chestnut
trees, there were very few intrusions into the low skyline until

you got the tower blocks around the city's fringes. There was the blue and white piping of the Pompidou Centre and of course the Tour Montparnasse, jabbed like a black glass dagger into the heart of Paris. But apart from that, the city seemed to be a collection of a million romantic garrets for budding Baudelaires to scribble away in. I couldn't prevent myself from smiling.

"It is a real visual cliché," Alexa groaned. [...]

"It's not a cliché for me, it's the first time I've been here."

"Hm," she grunted.

I turned away from the clichéd view. Keep her talking, I urged myself. What *does* she like?

"What did you think of *Amélie*?" I made telescope-focussing motions down towards the street a hundred feet or so below.

"Oh," she shrugged, "Jeunet is an intelligent director. But I preferred *Delicatessen*. Have you seen that?"

"No. What's it about?"

"What's it *about*?" She winced. This was apparently a film that was too good to be *about* anything. Another gaffe. "There were so many *close-ups* in *Amélie*." Alexa sounded outraged. "Half of the movie was just a poster of Audrey Tautou's eyes."

"Cute eyes, though," I tried to joke.

"Exactly," she huffed.

I suffered a moment of panic. Maybe, I thought, Alexa was under the impression I'd invited her out for a lesson in contemporary French aesthetics rather than a pre-bed snack.

Stephen Clarke, *A Year in the Merde*

* * *

If what you're after is something a little less 'personal' than a date with someone you actually know, then The Bluffer's Guide to Paris *has some sound information under the no-nonsense heading of 'Sex'.*

Paris has a reputation as a city of elegant sensuality, where sex and style go together to create a culture of studied, refined amorality; where the spectacles érotiques bear about as much resemblance to an East End pub Sunday lunchtime strip-tease as cordon bleu does to bubble and squeak. This is true, up to a point. But Paris's reputation as the place for acceptable naughtiness was made in the last century, and the rest of the world has done a lot of catching up. The classical symbols of Parisian decadent style, the **Moulin Rouge** and the **Folies Bergère** still exist (in the **Neuvième**, near Pigalle), but are unlikely to shock any but the most straight-laced – until, that is, they give you the bill.

It is no problem to find commercial erotic theatre of a more explicit nature – but it isn't really French, and is aimed much more at visitors. You should point this out. It does pay, however, to be aware of some of the sillier claims made for these establishments in their advertising, if only to be able to treat them with the tone of indulgent if world-weary amusement that befits the truly great bluffer. One such emporium states that 'le hard sans limites – ça existe', then in smaller letters, 'à St. Lazare'. Another establishment, on the rue des Ecoles, advertises live couples performing naked in nets over your head, which must be as uncomfortable for the couples as it is presumably damply unpleasant for the spectators. The proper attitude is to dismiss all these things, though for different reasons:

• The Moulin and the Folies are pale shadows of their former glories
• The newer clubs simply have nothing to do with anything genuinely French.

This line of nostalgia can usefully be pursued with the red-light districts as well, particularly that of rue **St. Denis**. What used to be a good, simple streetwalkers' street has been taken over by American bars and peep-shows; and regulars report the **filles** are not what they used to be either.

Jim Hankinson and Paul Bahn, *The Bluffer's Guide to Paris*

* * *

> *Given the right setting – and the right person wearing*
> *them – even a pair of shoes can titillate when the back-*
> *drop of the Paris art scene raises the sexual temperature*
> *… as in this scene from Kate Muir's novel,* Left Bank.

Scrunchity, scrunchity, scrunch went Madison's Christian
Louboutin heels across the gravel in the Musée Rodin garden
on the Rue de Varenne. The great advantage of Louboutin
shoes – aside from the fact that they give large feet a delicacy
previously only achieved by footbinding – is that their soles are
always scarlet red, allowing the beholder a sudden flash of the
forbidden. In the distance, Paul Rimbaud, director of the Musée
Rodin, was hormonally alerted by the signals from her shoes, the
modern equivalent of the red A for adulteress. Madison could
see Paul marvelling at the tiny cloud of dust raised around each
of her perfect ankles. He watched her walk down between the
espaliered apple trees until he could clearly no longer bear it.
Then he panted up beside her, like a respectful pug.

'From a curatorial standpoint, those red-soled sandals complete
you, in the way a red dot or a red handkerchief completes a
Corot painting,' he opened, pink with the heat and smiling from
ear to ear above his Paisley bow tie, pleased with his theory.

Madison leaned down and tenderly kissed Paul on both
cheeks; they were outside after all, and might be seen; why would
anyone expect more? Here they were, meeting in a public place,
where all who saw would know precisely their intent anyway.
But it being Paris, no one would make a fuss about it. Besides,
for Madison, there was as much pleasure in the anticipation,
the holding back, as there was in the release of the affair, and
she had no intention of consummating this one, ever. Lingering
was of some importance to a woman whose introduction to love
took place rapidly, regularly and roughly beneath the bleachers
of a Texas schoolyard with mosquitoes bloodsucking her back.

From behind one of the garden's statues, an overweight American tourist in a polyester tracksuit was videoing Madison with

her chignon and cinch-waisted suit as an example of perfect Parisian womanhood. Madison listened to her accent with a shiver of recognition that went back to her childhood, and realised that but a year or so and seventy pounds separated them as fellow Texans, one turned from cheerleader to beauty, the other to blubber. 'Darling, you look just fantastic,' said Paul, walking across the cameras sights, unaware. 'Are those new shoes?' He looked as though he might bend down to kiss her bare toes.

'Uh huh,' said Madison, all but ignoring his words. She marched briskly on and lit a Marlboro Light. 'Paul, darling, I have been thinking,' she said, blowing the smoke from pouting lips. 'I think I should start a salon in the Rue de Bac – you know, in the old-fashioned sense of Louise Colet, like we were talking about the other night, yet something modern, witty, a little bit dangerous. Halle, that half-Algerian poet, you know, might be a good start, and do you think, perhaps, Benedict Fournier would be an appropriate philosopher? You know, I read his *Ex-Tracts of Modernity* and I though that his line on Derrida was … '

'You would run the most adorable and, of course, intellectually significant salon,' said Paul, nodding, his glasses glinting with enthusiasm in the sunlight. 'You, and that wonderful apartment, would be a fantastic draw.' He took advantage of her concentration to slip his arm round her waist. Madison continued, oblivious. Her thin shadow moved along the gravel beside Paul's squat one.

Kate Muir, Left Bank

❊ ❊ ❊

A high-society, turn-of-the-century version of sex in the back of a car would be this famous scene from Swann in Love, *the second volume of Marcel Proust's* In Search of Lost Time. *After a miserable evening of going from restaurant to restaurant in his search for Odette, the high-class prostitute with whom he is hopelessly in love but has not yet so much as kissed, Swann finally catches up with her.*

He climbed after her into the carriage which she had kept waiting, and ordered his own to follow.

She had in her hand a bunch of cattleyas, and Swann could see, beneath the film of lace that covered her head, more of the same flowers fastened to a swansdown plume. She was wearing, under her cloak, a flowing gown of black velvet, caught up on one side so as to reveal a large triangle of white silk skirt, and with a yoke, also of white silk, in the cleft of the low-necked bodice, in which were fastened a few more cattleyas. She had scarcely recovered from the shock which the sight of Swann had given her, when some obstacle made the horse start to one side. They were thrown forward in their seats; she uttered a cry, and fell back quivering and breathless.

"It's all right," he assured her, "don't be frightened." And he slipped his arm around her shoulder, supporting her body against his own. Then went on: "Whatever you do, don't utter a word; just make a sign, yes or no, or you'll be out of breath again. You won't mind if I straighten the flowers on your bodice? The jolt has disarranged them. I'm afraid of their dropping out, so I'd just like to fasten them a little more securely."

She was not used to being made so much fuss of by men, and she smiled as she answered: "No, not at all; I don't mind in the least."

But he, daunted a little by her answer, and also, perhaps, to bear out the pretence that he had been sincere in adopting the stratagem, or even because he was already beginning to believe that he had been, exclaimed: "No, no, you mustn't speak. You'll get out of breath again. You can easily answer in signs; I shall understand. Really and truly now, you don't mind my doing this? Look, there is a little – I think it must be pollen, spilt over your dress. Do you mind if I brush it off with my hand? That's not too hard? I'm not hurting you, am I? Perhaps I'm tickling you a bit? I don't want to touch the velvet in case I crease it. But you see, I really had to fasten the flowers; they would have fallen out if I hadn't. Like that, now; if I just tuck them a little farther down ... Seriously, I'm not annoying you, am I? And if I just sniff them to see whether they've really got no scent? I don't believe I ever smelt any before. May I? Tell the truth, now."

Still smiling, she shrugged her shoulders ever so slightly, as who should say, "You're quite mad; you know very well that I like it."

He ran his other hand upward along Odette's cheek; she gazed at him fixedly, with that languishing and solemn air which marks the women of the Florentine master in whose faces he had found a resemblance with hers; swimming at the brink of eyelids, her brilliant eyes, wide and slender like theirs, seemed on the verge of welling out like two great tears. She bent her neck, as all their necks may be seen to bend, in the pagan scenes as well as the religious pictures. And in an attitude that was doubtless habitual to her, one which she knew to be appropriate to such moments and was careful not to forget to assume, she seemed to need all her strength to hold her face back, as though some invisible force were drawing it down towards Swann's. And Swann it was who, before she allowed it, as though in spite of herself, to fall upon his lips, held it back for a moment longer, at a little distance, between his hands.

Marcel Proust, *In Search of Lost Time*

* * *

Perhaps even more famous than Swann and Odette were the Parisian lovers of the twelfth century, Heloise and Abelard. He was a man of the church and already a respected teacher and philosopher when he became tutor to a young woman whose intellectual gifts were astonishing by any standards, but particularly for a female in medieval France. Peter Abelard's own account of their passionate affair and its painful outcome is frank and moving. They are buried together in a mock-gothic, canopied tomb in Père-Lachaise cemetery.

There was in Paris at the time a young girl named Heloise, the niece of Fulbert, one of the canons, and so much loved by him that he had done everything in his power to advance her education in letters. In looks she did not rank lowest, while in the extent of her learning she stood supreme. A gift for letters is so rare in women that it added greatly to her charm and had won her renown throughout the realm. I considered all the usual attractions for a lover and decided she was the one to bring to my bed, confident that I should have an easy success; for at that time I had youth and exceptional good looks as well as my great reputation to recommend me, and feared no rebuff from any woman I might choose to honour with my love. Knowing the girl's knowledge and love of letters I thought she would be all the more ready to consent, and that even when separated we could enjoy each other's presence by exchange of written messages in which we could speak more openly than in person, and so need never lack the pleasures of conversation.

All on fire with desire for this girl I sought an opportunity of getting to know her through private daily meetings and so more easily winning her over; and with this end in view I came to an arrangement with her uncle, with the help of some of his friends, whereby he should take me into his house, which was very near my school, for whatever sum he liked to ask. As a pretext I said that my household cares were hindering my studies and the expense was more than I could afford. Fulbert dearly loved money, and was moreover always ambitious to further his niece's education in letters, two weaknesses which made it easy for me to gain his consent and obtain my desire: he was all eagerness for my money and confident that his niece would profit from my teaching. This led him to make an urgent request which furthered my love and fell in with my wishes more than I had dared to hope; he gave me complete charge over the girl, so that I could devote all the leisure time left me by my school to teaching her by day and night, and if I found her idle I was to punish her severely. I was amazed by his simplicity – if he had entrusted a tender lamb to a ravening wolf it would not have surprised me more. In handing her over to me to punish as well as to teach, what else was he doing but giving me complete freedom to realize my desires, and providing an opportunity, even if I did not make use of it, for me to bend her to my will by threats and blows if persuasion failed? But there were two special reasons for his freedom from base suspicion: his love for his niece and my previous reputation for continence.

Need I say more? We were united in love, first under one roof, then in heart; and so with our lessons as a pretext we abandoned ourselves entirely to love. Her studies allowed us to withdraw in private, as love desired, and then with our books open before us, more words of love than of our reading passed between us, and more kissing than teaching. My hands strayed oftener to her bosom than to the pages; love drew our eyes to look on each other more than reading kept them on our texts. To avert suspicion I sometimes struck her, but these blows were prompted by love and tender feeling rather than anger and irritation, and were sweeter than any balm could be. In short, our desires left no stage of love-making untried, and if love could devise something new, we welcomed it. We entered on each joy the more eagerly for our previous inexperience, and were the less easily sated.[...]

Imagine the uncle's grief at the discovery, and the lovers' grief too at being separated! How I blushed with shame and contrition for the girl's plight, and what sorrow she suffered at the thought of my disgrace! All our laments were for one another's troubles, and our distress was for each other, not for ourselves. Separation drew our hearts still closer while frustration inflamed our passion even more; then we became more abandoned as we lost all sense of shame and, indeed, shame diminished as we found more opportunities for love-making. And so we were caught in the act as the poet says happened to Mars and Venus. Soon afterwards the girl found that she was pregnant, and immediately wrote me a letter full of rejoicing to ask what I thought she should do. One night then, when her uncle was away from home, I removed her secretly from his house, as we had planned, and sent her straight to my own country. There she stayed with my sister until she gave birth to a boy, whom she called Astralabe.

On his return her uncle went almost out of his mind – one could appreciate only by experience his transports of grief and mortification. What action could he take against me? What traps could he set? If he killed me or did me personal injury, there was the danger that his beloved niece might suffer for it in my country. It was useless to try to seize me or confine me anywhere against my will, especially as I was very much on guard against this very thing, knowing that he would not hesitate to assault me if he had the courage or the means.

In the end I took pity on his boundless misery and went to him, accusing myself of the deceit love had made me commit as if it were the basest treachery. I begged his forgiveness and promised to make any amends he might think fit. I protested that I had done nothing unusual in the eyes of anyone who had known the power of love, and recalled how since the beginning of the human race women had brought the noblest men to ruin. Moreover, to conciliate him further, I offered him satisfaction in a form he could never have hoped for: I would marry the girl I had wronged. All I stipulated was that the marriage should be kept secret so as not to damage my reputation. He agreed, pledged his word and that of his supporters, and sealed the reconciliation I desired with a kiss. But his intention was to make it easier to betray me.

I set off at once for Brittany and brought back my mistress to make her my wife. But she was strongly opposed to the proposal, and argued hotly against it for two reasons: the risk involved and the disgrace to myself. She swore that no satisfaction could ever appease her uncle, as we subsequently found out. [...]

Heloise then went on to the risks I should run in bringing her back, and argued that the name of mistress instead of wife would be dearer to her and more honourable for me – only love freely given should keep me for her, not the constriction of a marriage tie, and if we had to be parted for a time, we should find the joy of being together all the sweeter the rarer our meetings were. But at last she saw that her attempts to persuade or dissuade me were making no impression on my foolish obstinacy, and she could not bear to offend me; so amidst deep sighs and tears she ended in these words: 'We shall both be destroyed. All that is left us is suffering as great as our love has been.' In this, as the whole world knows, she showed herself a true prophet.

And so when our baby son was born we entrusted him to my sister's care and returned secretly to Paris. A few days later, after a night's private vigil of prayer in a certain church, at dawn we were joined in matrimony in the presence of Fulbert and some of his, and our, friends. Afterwards we parted secretly and went our ways unobserved. Subsequently our meetings were few and furtive, in order to conceal as far as possible what we had done. But Fulbert and his servants, seeking satisfaction for the dishonour done to him, began to spread the news of the marriage and break the promise of secrecy they had given me. Heloise cursed them and swore there was no truth in this, and in his exasperation Fulbert heaped abuse on her on several occasions. As soon as I discovered this I removed her to a convent of nuns in the town near Argenteuil, where she had been brought up and educated as a small girl, and I also had made for her a religious habit of the type worn by novices, with the exception of the veil, and made her put it on.

At this news her uncle and his friends and relatives imagined that I had tricked them, and had found myself an easy way of ridding myself of Heloise by making her a nun. Wild with indignation they plotted against me, and one night as I slept peacefully in an inner room in my lodgings, they bribed one of my servants to admit them and there took cruel vengeance on me of such appalling barbarity as to shock the whole world; they cut off the parts of my body whereby I had committed the wrong of which they complained.

They then fled, but the two who could be caught were blinded and mutilated as I had been, one of them being the servant who had been led by greed while in my service to betray his master.

Peter Abelard, Historia calamitatum or Story of his misfortunes,
translated by Betty Radice

✽ ✽ ✽

Longing. Nostalgia. Lost loves. Regrets. Anguished memories of bodies that no longer share our bed ... Paris is as good for that as for more joyful sexual experiences. At the opening of Hopscotch, *by Argentinian-born but Paris-based writer Julio Cortázar (1914–1984), the narrative voice addresses a young woman – a former lover – whose presence he longs for as he haunts the roads and bridges of Paris.*

Why was I coming to the Pont des Arts? It seems to me that on that Thursday in December I had intended to cross over to the Right Bank to have some wine in a little café on the Rue des Lombards where Madame Léonie reads my palm and tells me of trips and surprises. I never took you to have your palm read by Madame Léonie, probably because I was afraid she would read some truth about me in your hand, because you have always been a frightful mirror, a monstrous instrument of repetitions, and what we had called loving was perhaps my standing in front of you holding a yellow flower while you held two green candles and a slow rain of renunciations and farewells and Métro tickets blew into our faces. So I never took you to Madame Léonie's, Maga. You told me so and that is how I know that you did not like my watching you go into that little bookshop on the Rue de Verneuil, where a burdened old man fills out thousands of reference cards and knows everything there is to know about the study of history. You used to go there to play with a cat, and the old man let you in and didn't ask questions, content for you to get him a book from time to time from the upper shelves. You used to get warm at that stove of his with its big black chimney, and you didn't like me to know that you were going to sit next to that stove. But all of this should have been said in its proper time, except that it was difficult to know what the proper time for things was, and even now, with my elbows on the railing of the bridge, as I watched a small, must-coloured *péniche*, sparkling clean like a great big beautiful cockroach, with a woman in a white apron hanging washing on a wire strung along the prow, as I looked at its windows, painted green, with Hansel and Gretel curtains, even now, Maga, I wondered if this roundabout route made any sense, since it would have been easier to reach the Rue des Lombards by the Pont Saint-Michel and the Pont au Change. But if you had been there that night, as so many other times, then I would have known that the roundabout made sense, while now, on the other hand, I debase my failure by calling it a roundabout. I raised the collar of my lumber-jacket, and it was a matter of going along by the docks until I came to where the large shops finish at the Châtelet, passing underneath the violet shadow of the Tour Saint-Jacques, and turning into my street, thinking about the fact that I had not bumped into you and about Madame Léonie.

I know that one day I came to Paris. I know that I was living in hock for a while, doing what the others did and seeing what they saw. I know that you were coming out of a café on the Rue du Cherche-Midi and that we spoke. [...] I followed you grudgingly then, finding you petulant and rude, until you got tired of not being tired and we went into a café on the Boul' Mich' and all of a sudden in between two croissants you told me a whole chunk of your life.

How could I have suspected that what seemed to be a pack of lies was all true, a Figari with sunset violets, with livid faces, with hunger and blows in the corners. I came to believe you later on, later on there was reason to, there was Madame Léonie, who looked at my hand which had gone to bed with your breasts, and she practically repeated your exact words: "She is suffering somewhere. She has always suffered. She is very cheerful, she adores yellow, her bird is the blackbird, her time is night, her bridge is the Pont des Arts." (A must-coloured *péniche*, Maga, and I wonder why we didn't sail off on it while there was still time.) […]

We used to eat hamburgers in the Carrefour de l'Odéon and we went cycling to Montparnasse, to any hotel, any pillow. Then other times we would go all the way to the Porte d'Orléans and we became more and more familiar with the vacant lots beyond the Boulevard Jourdan, where sometimes at midnight the members of the Serpent Club used to get together to talk to a blind seer, a stimulating paradox. We used to leave the bicycles on the street and go in a little way, stopping to look at the sky because it is one of the few places in Paris where sky is worth more than ground. Sitting on a pile of rubbish we would smoke for a while, and La Maga would stroke my hair or hum songs which hadn't been invented yet, absurd tunes broken with sighs or memories.

Julio Cortázar, *Hopscotch*, translated by Gregory Rabassa

* * *

Another kind of search is undertaken by Jennifer Cox. Unable to find her ideal man and soul-mate in London, she sets off to search for him, travelling Around the World in 80 Dates. *When she meets a handsome, intelligent Parisian, she begins to think she's found what she was after …*

I was booked into a hotel in the Marais, my favourite Parisian neighbourhood. Touristy in parts, the area was mostly elegant and couture but, thankfully, its relentless chicness softened by pockets of pretty squares fringed with pungent fromageries and cafés stocked with casually fantastic pastries.

I rushed back and changed in a hurry: I had an hour before my next date.

Showered and dressed in my new baby-blue linen top (I had spotted a gorgeous boutique on the corner of my street and raced in on the way back from the metro), I took the short walk from my hotel to the Place des Vosges. This elegant square of houses dated back to 1612, and amongst its residents were Richelieu and Victor Hugo. The park at its centre was once used for duelling; tonight it would be used for dating: this was where I was to meet Olivier, Date # 12.

I was very curious about Olivier. He seemed extremely French: flawlessly educated and virulently contemptuous. He worked in the French film industry and would leave long gaps between emails as he (and he described it with 'pulling teeth' loathing) had to be at meetings everywhere from Brussels to Cannes. His emailed photos were taken from about 500 yards away, the only discernible features a crazy mop of dark hair and severe horn-rimmed glasses.

I was curious about him, but didn't feel I knew or had developed much of a rapport with him. He admitted in one email he could: *stay mute and prostrated for hours, not even noticing someone is sitting by my side ... depends on my mood ...*

This might have made me nervous but for the fact that the date had been set up by my friend Muriel, a smart, exuberant French woman living in London. I knew any friend of hers was going to be worth meeting.

It was a warm early summer's evening and the pavement cafés were already full of loquacious Parisians enjoying the sunshine and unhurriedly sipping glasses of red wine (the French were restrained enough to order wine by the glass – to the binge-drinking Brits this felt about as logical as buying a house by the room).

I spotted Olivier as soon as I walked into the park, but skirted around a statue so I could check him out before he saw me. First impression: tall, slim without being skinny, but glasses and hair – as in the photos – the dominant features. Was an evening with Olivier going to be hard work? I took a deep breath and stepped out from behind the statue to introduce myself.

As he turned to greet me, I was shocked by something I had not prepared myself for.

He was cute.

Under that mop of dark-brown curly hair and severe glasses, Olivier had gorgeous green eyes, freckled skin and a fine nose. I smiled instinctively: I'd been prepared for an interesting, possibly argumentative date; I was quick to revise my opinion and put my 'flirt face' on.

'Hi, I'm Jennifer,' I said unnecessarily (we'd both seen each other's photos), holding my hand out to shake his. Olivier's hand was warm and firm in mine. [...]

I tended not to get too nervous about the dates [...] However, because I hadn't expected Olivier to be good-looking – plus he was French so he didn't care what I thought anyway – I was caught off-guard and [...] launched into a manic account of how my mother and sister used to live in Paris and wasn't the weather great and wasn't Paris better than London because it was so much smaller and Oh I love the Marais, there are so many cute shops ... I listened with horror as the anecdotes and opinions poured uncontrollably out of me at top speed. Olivier studied me with an amused expression, which was all he could do as my jabbering made it impossible for him to get a word in.

[...] I stopped talking.

Olivier waited to see if I would start again. I didn't. So he smiled and asked: 'Would you like a drink?'

I nodded gratefully, we left the park and began our date.

It was a wonderful evening. Olivier and I wandered along the banks of the Seine, stopping for glasses of wine, dinner in a little bistro, coffee in a café by now lit by moonlight, whisky in a crowded after-hours bar ... We walked and talked through the romantic streets of the Marais; crossed the Seine to the touristy twists and turns of the Latin Quarter and back again through the crowded club-land of rue de Lappe and Bastille.

Olivier was every bit as challenging as I imagined and ten times as interesting. He had lived and studied all over Europe and was passionate about art and films. His personality was like a medieval city of switchback streets opening up into beautiful courtyards: impenetrable and magical in turns. And as he opened up, he became more tactile: touching my hand to make a point, standing close behind me and reaching over my shoulder to show me something fascinating and obscure about a building.

I had decided after Denmark that I was only going to stay out late or agree to see the date again if I felt he was a genuine prospect. It was now 3 a.m. and I still felt intrigued and utterly entertained by Olivier. I was also attracted to him and felt comfortable enough with the pace at which things were progressing to anticipate with pleasure the French Kiss that I was confident would come at the end of the date.

By 3.30 a.m., we were both completely talked out and I was glad when Olivier offered to walk me back to my hotel. I'd had a wonderful evening and felt really good about seeing him the next day if he asked. It was the perfect time to end the date.

Thirty minutes later, we stood together outside my hotel, our faces gently lit by the fading streetlights and the approaching dawn that now warmed the sky.

Olivier admitted, 'I really did not know what to expect from this evening, Jennifer, but it has been extremely enjoyable. It is unlike me to talk of myself so much; you are charming and very good company.' Studying me through his glasses, his eyes were dark and intent. He was about four inches taller than me, so when I told him how much I had enjoyed the evening too, I had to tilt my face up towards his to answer, smiling warmly into his eyes.

I watched his mouth as he talked: I was going to get kissed and I was feeling really good about it.

'If you have time, I would very much like to see you again tomorrow?' Olivier asked.

'I would like that too,' I replied simply.

Olivier smiled. 'It is agreed then.'

I relaxed. He smiled at me, I smiled at him. I waited happily, I was in no rush.

'Umm, okay, then I shall see you tomorrow,' Olivier suddenly blurted out and with an awkward half-shrug he turned and walked off down the street.

Huh?

I watched in astonishment as my cheeky-guy fun vanished around the corner. What had just happened? Why hadn't he kissed me? I shook my head vigorously, as if trying to shake some sense into it. I didn't understand: why hadn't he kissed me? We liked each other. He'd asked me out again. Why didn't he want to kiss me? Why?

I suddenly felt furious with him: how could he do this? I'd stayed out most of the night with him and would now undoubtedly spend the rest of the night wide awake, agonising over why he hadn't wanted to kiss me. I mean, I know he didn't have to, but I was really sure he'd wanted to. What terrible thing had I said or done that had made him change his mind? Could I isolate the thing which had made me an Unkissable?

One thing was certain: I had no intention of ever seeing him again.

Jennifer Cox, *Around the World in 80 Dates*

✤ ✤ ✤

After divorcing her first husband (who'd locked her in a room to write the instantly successful 'Claudine' books which he published under his own name), Colette worked as a music-hall artist. Her 1911 novel The Vagabond *is closely based on her experiences. Freed from the need to keep up appearances, she frequents the bars of Montmartre where the local prostitutes also go for their modest meals. Here she gives a moving and perceptive snapshot of such lives, the truth of it still recognisable today.*

'Come and have a bite at Olympe's this evening,' said Brague to me at the rehearsal. 'And afterwards we'll go and say hullo to the boys in the *Revue* at the Emp'-Clich'.'

There's no danger of my misunderstanding: this is not an *invitation* to dinner; we are two *comrades*, and the protocol – for there is one – governing comradeship between artistes banishes all ambiguity.

So I rejoin Brague this evening at Olympe's bar, whose doubtful reputation does not in the least disturb me. Now that I need give no thought to my own reputation, I feel neither apprehension nor pleasure when I enter this little Montmartre restaurant, which is silent from seven to ten and resounds all the rest of the night with what seems rather a deliberate din made up of shouts, the clatter of crockery, and the twanging of guitars. I sometimes used to go and dine there in haste, alone or with Brague, last month, before we went on to the Empyrée-Clichy.

This evening a waitress from the country, tranquil and slow in the midst of the calls for her, serves us with pickled pork and cabbage, a filling, nourishing dish, rather heavy for the stomachs of the poor little local prostitutes who sit eating near us, by themselves, with that aggressive look which animals and under-nourished women adopt when a heaped plate is put before them. No, indeed, the place is not always gay!

Brague, mocking but compassionate at heart, speaks slightingly of two thin young women who have just entered, with idiotic hats balanced precariously on their curly heads. One of them is striking, and carries her head with a kind of angry insolence; every line of her exaggerated slenderness shows, in all its grace, beneath a tight sheath of pink Liberty silk, bought from the second-hand clothes woman. On this freezing February evening all she has to cover her is a cloak, a sort of light cape, also of Liberty silk, blue and embroidered with tarnished silver. She is frozen, almost beside herself with cold, and her furious grey eyes repulse all compassion;

she is ready to insult, or even to claw, the first person who says to her, sympathetically, 'Poor child!'

Young women of this kind, slowly dying of misery and pride, beautiful in their stark poverty, are by no means uncommon in this district of Montmartre. I meet them here and there, trailing their flimsy garments from table to table at supper-time on the Butte, gay, drunk, and fierce, always ready to bite, never gentle, never affectionate, resenting their profession and 'working' all the same. The men call them 'wretched little sluts', with a contemptuous but admiring laugh, because they belong to a breed which never gives in, never admits to cold or hunger or love; little sluts who die saying: 'I'm not ill,' who may bleed under blows, but hit back all the same.

Yes, I know something of those girls, and it is of them that I am reminded as I watch the proud, frozen young girl who has just come into Olympe's.

A hungry half-silence reigns in the bar. Two painted young men exchange barbed repartee from opposite ends of the room, without any conviction. A street-girl with short legs, who is dining on a crème-de-menthe with water while awaiting a problematical supper, throws out a few half-hearted retorts. A bulldog bitch, in pup to bursting point, pants painfully on the threadbare carpet, her balloon of a stomach studded with knob-like teats.

Colette, The Vagabond, translated by Enid McLeod

✻ ✻ ✻

High Hopes ... and hard times

Paris has long been a magnet for artists, writers, composers, thinkers ... and vaguely hopeful and ambitious young men and women of all kinds. The first three excerpts in this section each features a young man getting to grips with Paris and feeling all the wonderful possibilities of the life before them. The narrator of Julian Barnes' early novel, Metroland, *finds himself there in 1968. Journalist Walter Schwarz, for ten years the* Guardian *correspondent in Paris, recovers his 17-year-old self through letters home during an extended stay in Paris. And in a short story, Adam Thorpe's young American heads straight for the Latin Quarter, full of dreams, excitement ... and loneliness.*

I'd already been to Paris many times before 1968, and didn't go with any of the naïve expectations Toni was greedy to attribute to me. I'd already done the Paree side of it in my late teens; green Olympia Press paperbacks, ocular loitering from boulevard cafés, thrusting leather G-strings and pouches in a Montparnasse simulation-dive. I'd done the city-as-history bit while a student, I-spying the famous in Père Lachaise, and coming back exultant over an unexpected find: the catacombs at Denfert-Rochereau, where post-Revolutionary history and personal glooming could be sweetly combined as you wandered among the vaults of transplanted skeletons, sorted and stacked by bone rather than body: neat banks of femurs and solid cubes of skulls suddenly rose up before the groping light of your candle. I'd even, by this time, stopped sneering at my exhausted compatriots who clogged the cafés round the Gare du Nord, waving fingers to indicate the number of Pernods they wanted.

I chose Paris because it was a familiar place where I could, if I wanted to, live alone. I knew the city; I knew the language; I wouldn't be harassed by the food or the climate. It was too large to have a menacingly hospitable colony of English émigrés. There would be little to stop me concentrating on myself.

I was lent a flat up in Buttes-Chaumont (the clanking 7-*bis* Métro line: Bolivar, Buttes-Chaumont, Botzaris) by a friend-of-a-friend. It was an airy, slightly derelict studio-bedroom with a creaky French floor and a fruit machine in the corner which worked off a supply of old francs kept on a shelf. In the kitchen was a rack of home-made calvados which I was allowed to drink provided I replaced each bottle with a substitute one of whisky (I lost money on the deal, but gained local colour).

I installed my few possessions, greased up to the concierge, Mme Huet, in her den of house-plants and diarrhoeic cats and back numbers of *France Dimanche* (she tipped me off about each *nouvelle intervention chirurgicale à Windsor*), registered at the Bibliothèque Nationale (which wasn't too conveniently close) and began to fancy myself, at long last, as an autonomous being. [...]

I walked to the Palais Royal feeling impressed with myself. I sat on a bench in the courtyard and inhaled the warm night. I felt as if everything was coming together, all at once. The past was all around; I was the present; art was here, and history, and now the promise of something much like love or sex. Over there in that corner was where Molière worked; across there, Cocteau, then Colette; there Blücher lost six million at roulette and for the rest of his life flew into a rage when the name of Paris was mentioned; there the first *café méchanique* was opened; and there, over there, at a little cutler's in the Galerie de Valois, Charlotte Corday bought the knife with which she killed Marat. And bringing it all together, ingesting it, making it mine, was me – fusing all the art and the history with what I might soon, with luck, be calling life. The

Gautier which Toni and I quoted to each other at school sidled into my head – '*Tout passe*', it murmured. Maybe, I replied, but not for quite a bloody long time; not if I have anything to do with it.

Julian Barnes, *Metroland*

* * *

I was 17 when Father gave me a stupendous present. With my Higher School Certificate in the bag I had six free months before university entrance exams. His fantastic idea was to arrange, through old French friends of his, for me to spend those six months in Paris.

This was 1947. Food was rationed, Parisians queued for bread and beggars played their accordions. Mass tourism had not been invented and 17-year-olds were still children, yet here I was, venturing abroad alone – and to Paris! This was high adventure from the moment the train moved out of Piccadilly station.

I was to be under the protection of father's old friends the Hervés who lived in Montmartre, but they had arranged for me to stay with Mademoiselle de Lessert, a genteel, impoverished old lady in the rue de la Faisanderie in the affluent *16e arrondissement*, a few minutes walk from the Bois de Boulogne. The family kept all my voluminous letters and I kept all theirs.

"The truth of the matter is that I have settled down in Paris and become a Parisian," I wrote at the end of my first week.

13 June 1947
Speaking French to strangers has become part of the natural order of things ... . It is no longer a nightmarish adventure to take a ride in the metro or ask someone for information. I sit reading a newspaper without bothering to look up, for I know all the stations between Porte Dauphine and Jules-Joffrin. It does take some time for the smiling spaciousness of the streets to sink in ... . It is wonderful to live in a beautiful street. At one end are the Avenues Victor Hugo and Henri Martin – the one with its white, young trees on either side and the Arc de Triomphe

visible at the end (about a mile away) and the other with its double line of trees in the centre, curving gracefully into the Bois and at its other end is the Avenue Foch ... Just imagine me going out to do my shopping in the Ave Victor Hugo instead of Burton Road! ... There is no need to describe to my Parisian father the breathtaking beauty of such things as the view from the Place du Carousel to the Etoile, as the Jardin des Tuileries, as the Bois de Boulogne, as Notre Dame, as the view from the Trocadéro ... .

The Hervés had a big apartment just under the Sacré Coeur where they could not, in my eyes, have been more French.
16 June 1947
The dinners are splendid affairs. Usually there are four different sorts of wine at each evening. One starts the evening with an aperitif, then one has two successive table wines (several glasses of each) and then one has some exquisite liqueur. I hope you don't mind me smoking occasionally now. It steadies me after all the wine and makes me feel much more sociable ... To return to the dinners – they are superb. I like particularly the vegetables, which are – as you know – eaten apart from the meat. The evenings are always very jolly affairs with all sorts of interesting people.

[...] I went to concerts at the Salle Gaveau and wrote critiques to my family, who reciprocated with news of the latest recitals in Manchester.

15 July 1947
New friends: 1. One of the best-known young French pianists – called Wilfred Maggiar . Great friend of the Hervés, where I met him. A very nice chap, not conceited. He likes me, and we see each other a lot. He plays to me often in his studio at the Salle Gaveau (to me alone, and whatever I ask for). He says I am "très musicien" and "très sympathique." We also went to Versailles together to visit the Château. He is going to make a tour in England in November which will include Manchester and he'll probably play with the Hallé. He has 18 concertos in his repertoire

including the Emperor, the Schumann, Brahms 2nd, Tchaikovsky,
and the C.Frank Variations which he plays to me. But he plays
mostly Chopin. He is half English and speaks English perfectly.

2. Another chap I met is a Tunisian student called Bourguiba,
nephew of the Tunisian nationalist leader. He hates the French
and maintains that what the French do in Tunisia is just as bad
as what the Nazis ever did, only it is concealed from the outside
world by an iron curtain. He lives for the day when the French
will clear out, and belongs to a society with that object in view.

An interesting thing about this chap Bourguiba is where he lives.
It's a big student hostel which, just six months ago, was an official
brothel. Signs are still up on the walls of the rooms with instruc-
tions on precautions against disease. There is also a big hall lit up in
red where the girls were on display for people to choose. I thought
this was very funny – a bit of real Parisian life. But don't worry, all
that is gone. I go out with this young man quite a lot ... .

Wilfred Maggiar took a very great fancy to me indeed and we
spent a lot of time together. He was a warm, frank, emotional
man. The two of us stayed for a few days in a studio flat in the
magnificent Place des Vosges, where I slept chastely on a mattress
on the floor. Wilfred among other things was a gentleman.

1, Place des Vosges Paris 4e. Saturday 11 September 1947.

Wilfred was here to receive me on Wednesday evening in this
charming little "studio" in this charming square which consists
entirely of 17th Century buildings – similar huge blocks on
each of the four sides which are today exactly as they were
in the 17th Century. As we live on the sixth floor we have a
splendid view of the square which has a park in the centre and
a statue of Louis XIII in the centre of that. ...

The life we lead here is bohemian in the extreme. The owner
of the studio is a poet ... . [...] Wilfred is very charming with
his 100% artist's temperament, his frank and simple manner –
curiously combined with an immense conceit. ... When I am

alone I spend a lot of the time in the Louvre, or just walking
about, which is the best thing to do in Paris.

Walter Schwarz, *The Ideal Occupation*

* * *

I made straight for the Latin Quarter. The tug-boats were
hooting and the cobbles were wet and slippery, the light mist
made everything almost industrial. It was a weird moment.
There were ragged humps with bottles lying in the lee of the
quai, mumbling or snorting, and a few guys fishing off the bank
down below. There was someone getting their poodle to swim,
but it didn't like it. The first leaves were dropping. Smart women
walked by with their dogs, both species with their noses in the
air. The women were muffled in furs but still elegant on high
heels, clicking past me one after the other as I advanced with a
beating heart toward what I could only think of as my destiny.

The cold and wet of Paris was soaking in. I mussed my hair,
but it was too short to muss properly. As I crossed the place Saint
Michel I vowed to grow it long. Then I had to consult my tourist
map. It was given to me at the hotel where I was staying until I
found suitable lodgings. My hotel was on the quai d'Orsay. In
those days suitable rooms could be rented cheap even on the
quai d'Orsay. As I struggled with my map in the wind off the
river, trying to figure out exactly where the Latin Quarter started
in case I missed it, I pictured this garret and me inside it, painting
or writing poetry. I was stained with oil paints, ink, the juices of
the streets and boulevards, you name it. I was *living*.

Not clean-living but *dirty*-living. Europe was old and dirty, we
all knew that. That's why my fellow Americans were such notorious tenants: they left their apartments looking dirty and broken
because that's what they thought Europe expected. No one else
could figure this out, but I could. A cream-and-blue bus, open at
the back, flicked its tyres over the wet cobbles, *flicker-flacker-flick-
er-flacker-flicker-flacker-flick* – one of those crazy Parisian mating

calls of the old days. I responded. The map crumpled in my hands. I knew where the Latin Quarter was: it was in my heart.

I was feeling really mushy by now, so I stopped at the first café I came across, near Saint Severin, and ordered a coffee and a pastry. The place was almost empty, but it was warm. I was so green that I tipped the waiter. We Americans still think that money buys smiles, but all it does is spoil the fruit of the soul. Then I explored, looking around for this hill, the garret, some tight buttons to fumble at inside my head. I liked the little dead-end alleys most of all. Paris was darker in those days, blacker, it had a deep smell of drains, there was undifferentiated poverty, a shabby-genteel joy that had drawn itself out like a greasy greatcoat's thread all the way from the nineteenth century. Everyone old back then in the fifties was not of our world, they were born elsewhere, in some other time, before technology and American ease and the glide of cars. This guy with the white hair, he might have passed Mallarmé or Baudelaire. That old dame with the moustache, she might have slept with Auguste Rodin. Rimbaud or Verlaine or both at once might have heard this legless guy blowing his flute through his nose.

I remember that legless guy, he was there most days that year, I got used to him like I've got used to wealthy nuts in a thousand divorce cases since. But he'd jerk his head like a maniac and I couldn't stand the sound that first time, the guy looked like a grub, he was completely bald, all you could see was the top of his glistening head. They were washing the street and the soapy water sailed past his stumps, making a stream between us. There was the damp, soapy smell of a Sunday morning in Paris, with grey-black buildings and somebody singing high up and this jerky head with a flute stuck in one nostril, wailing and whistling over alien shouts down the street. There was me, fumbling for foreign coins, feeling so young and American and excited and lonely and disgusted all at the same time. Frightened, even. Frightened by the prospect of so much life in front of me ...

Adam Thorpe, Shifts

* * *

> *Marya, the protagonist of Jean Rhys's 1928 novel*
> Quartet, *has few illusions about 'la vie parisienne'.*
> *Even in Paris, hard times are hard times.*

It was about half-past five on an October afternoon when Marya Zelli came out of the Café Lavenue, which is a dignified and comparatively expensive establishment on the Boulevard du Montparnasse. She had been sitting there for nearly an hour and a half, and during that time she had drunk two glasses of black coffee, smoked six caporal cigarettes and read the week's *Candide*.

Marya was a blonde girl, not very tall, slender-waisted. Her face was short, high cheek-boned, full-lipped; her long eyes slanted upwards towards the temples and were gentle and oddly remote in expression. Often on the Boulevards St Michel and Montparnasse shabby youths would glide up to her and address her hopefully in unknown and spitting tongues. When they were very shabby she would smile in a distant manner and answer in English:

'I'm very sorry; I don't understand what you are saying.'

She crossed the boulevard and turned down the Rue de Rennes. As she walked along she was thinking: 'This street is very like the Tottenham Court Road – own sister to the Tottenham Court Road.'

The idea depressed her, and to distract herself she stopped to look at a red felt hat in a shop window. Someone behind her said:

'Hello, Madame Zelli, what are you doing in this part of the world?'

Miss Esther De Solla, tall, gaunt, broad-shouldered, stood looking downwards at her with a protective expression. When Marya answered: 'Hello! Nothing. I was feeling melancholy, to tell you the truth,' she proposed:

'Come along to my studio for a bit.'

Miss De Solla, who was a painter and ascetic to the point of fanaticism, lived in a street at the back of the Lion de Belfort.

Her studio was hidden behind a grim building where the house-wives of the neighbourhood came to wash their clothes. It was a peaceful place, white-walled, smelling strongly of decayed vegetables. The artist explained that a *marchand des quatre saisons* kept her stock in the courtyard, and that as the woman was the concierge's sister-in-law, complaints were useless.

'Though the smell's pretty awful sometimes. Sit near the stove. It's cold today.'

She opened a massive cupboard and produced a bottle of gin, another of vermouth, two glasses and a cardboard case containing drawings.

'I bought these this morning. What do you think of them?'

Marya, helped by the alcohol, realized that the drawings were beautiful. Groups of women. Masses of flesh arranged to form intricate and absorbing patterns.

'That man's a Hungarian,' explained Miss De Solla. 'He's just over the way in the house where Trotsky used to live. He's a discovery of Heidler's. You know Heidler, the English picture-dealer man, of course.'

Marya answered: 'I don't know any of the English people in Paris.'

'Don't you?' said Miss De Solla, shocked. Then she added hastily: 'How perfectly lovely for you!'

'Do you think so?' asked Marya, dubiously.

Miss De Solla assured her that it was.

'I do think that one ought to make an effort to get away from the Anglo-Saxons in Paris, or what on earth is the good of being here at all? And it isn't an easy thing to do, either. Not easy for a woman, anyhow. But, of course, your husband's French, isn't he?'

'No,' said Marya. 'He's a Pole.'

The other looked across at her and thought: 'Is she really married to the Zelli man, I wonder? She's a decorative little person – decorative but strangely pathetic. I must get her to sit for me.'

73

She began to argue that there was something unreal about most English people.

'They touch life with gloves on. They're pretending about something all the time. Pretending quite nice and decent things, of course. But still ... '

'Everybody pretends,' Marya was thinking. 'French people pretend every bit as much, only about different things and not so obviously. She'll know that when she's been here as long as I have.'

'As long as I have.' The four years she had spent in Paris seemed to stretch into infinity.

'English people ... ' continued Miss De Solla in a dogmatic voice.

The drone of a concertina sounded from the courtyard of the studio. The man was really trying to play "Yes, we have no bananas". But it was an unrecognizable version, and listening to it gave Marya the same feeling of melancholy pleasure as she had when walking along the shadowed side of one of those narrow streets full of shabby *parfumeries*, second-hand book-stalls, cheap hat-shops, bars frequented by gaily-painted ladies and loud-voiced men, midwives' premises ...

Montparnasse was full of these streets and they were often inordinately long. You could walk for hours. The Rue Vaugirard, for instance. Marya had never yet managed to reach the end of the Rue Vaugirard, which was a very respectable thoroughfare on the whole. But if you went far enough towards Grenelle and then turned down side streets ...

Only the day before she had discovered, in this way, a most attractive restaurant. There was no *patronne*, but the *patron* was beautifully made up. Crimson was where crimson should be, and rose-colour where rose-colour. He talked with a lisp. The room was full of men in caps who bawled intimacies at each other; a gramophone played without ceasing; a beautiful white dog under the counter, which everybody called Zaza and threw bones to, barked madly.

But Stephan objected with violence to these wanderings in sordid streets. And though Marya considered that he was extremely inconsistent, she generally gave way to his inconsistencies and spent hours alone in the bedroom of the Hôtel de l'Univers. Not that she objected to solitude. Quite the contrary. She had books, thank Heaven, quantities of books. All sorts of books.

Still, there were moments when she realized that her existence, though delightful, was haphazard. It lacked, as it were, solidity; it lacked the necessary fixed background. A bedroom, balcony and *cabinet de toilette* in a cheap Montmartre hotel cannot possibly be called a solid background.

Jean Rhys, Quartet

✻ ✻ ✻

Another insalubrious hotel in a poor part of Paris is vividly depicted, a few years later than Jean Rhys, by George Orwell. He deliberately set out to experience the life of the poor in Paris and London. His observations are vivid and revealing, but perhaps without the same despair and urgency of the genuinely poor.

The rue du Coq d'Or, Paris, seven in the morning. A succession of furious, choking yells from the street. Madame Monce, who kept the little hotel opposite mine, had come out onto the pavement to address a lodger on the third floor. Her bare feet were stuck into sabots and her grey hair was streaming down.

MADAME MONCE: '*Salope! Salope!* How many times have I told you not to squash bugs on the wallpaper? Do you think you've bought the hotel, eh? Why can't you throw them out of the window like everyone else? *Putain! Salope!*'

THE WOMAN ON THE THIRD FLOOR: '*Vache!*'

Thereupon a whole variegated chorus of yells, as windows were flung open on every side and half the street joined in the quarrel. They shut up abruptly ten minutes later, when a squadron of cavalry rode past and people stopped shouting to look at them.

I sketch this scene, just to convey something of the spirit of the rue du Coq d'Or. Not that quarrels were the only thing that happened there – but still, we seldom got through the morning without at least one outburst of this description. Quarrels, and the desolate cries of street hawkers, and the shouts of children chasing orange-peel over the cobbles, and at night loud singing and the sour reek of the refuse-carts, made up the atmosphere of the street.

It was a very narrow street – a ravine of tall, leprous houses, lurching towards one another in queer attitudes, as though they had all been frozen in the act of collapse. All the houses were hotels and packed to the tiles with lodgers, mostly Poles, Arabs and Italians. At the foot of the hotels were tiny *bistros*, where you could be drunk for the equivalent of a shilling. On Saturday nights about a third of the male population of the quarter was drunk. There was fighting over women, and the Arab navvies who lived in the cheapest hotels used to conduct mysterious feuds, and fight them out with chairs and occasionally revolvers. At night the policemen would only come through the street two together. It was a fairly rackety place. And yet amid the noise and dirt lived the usual respectable French shopkeepers, bakers and laundresses and the like, keeping themselves to themselves and quietly piling up small fortunes. It was quite a representative Paris slum. [...]

There were eccentric characters in the hotel. The Paris slums are a gathering-place for eccentric people – people who have fallen into solitary, half-mad grooves of life and given up trying to be normal or decent. Poverty frees them from ordinary standards of behaviour, just as money frees people from work. Some of the lodgers in our hotel lived lives that were curious beyond words.

There were the Rougiers, for instance, an old, ragged, dwarfish couple who plied an extraordinary trade. They used to sell post-cards on the Boulevard St Michel. The curious thing was that the postcards were sold in sealed packets as pornographic ones, but they were actually photographs of chateaux on the Loire; the buyers did not discover this till too late, and of course they never complained.

George Orwell, *Down and Out in Paris and London*

✻ ✻ ✻

There are, and always have been, plenty of people
trying to scrape a living on the streets of Paris. In
John Williams' short story 'New Shoes', a middle-
aged man drinking on the famous rue Mouffetard
recalls his youth as a busker.

In the spring of 1981 there were only three places in Paris to
busk. The first and easily the best, probably the best place in
all Europe, was outside the Beaubourg. Can I start to explain
how fabulous the Beaubourg was back then? This building
with its primary-coloured plumbing on the outside, with its
giant Perspex escalator clambering across the front. I can
hardly credit it myself – twenty-five years of living in this city
has allowed familiarity to do the job of breeding contempt –
but really back then it seemed to represent a whole world of
possibilities, a future in which anything could happen. We'd
lost sight of that you see, in those first years of Thatcher, living
in a city, Cardiff, that was closing down around us.

But back to the point. There were three places to busk in Paris
that spring, and the big open space in front of the Beauborg,
always full of tourists and locals marvelling at the this new
wonder, was by far the best of them. The others were the Métro
and the rue St André des Arts, but each of those had its problems, as we discovered.

Who were we? We were seven. No eight, refugees from the
punk-rock experience, boys and girls hoping to shift our lives
from black and white into technicolor. We'd pooled our dole
money and student grants and wages from the anarchist print
shop and crammed into the back of my old Transit van and
headed to Paris to busk. Our act, such as it was, consisted of
playing hits of the day – David Bowie, Adam and the Ants,
Robert Wyatt, whatever – in ragged vocal harmony style backed
only by percussion and kazoos. At the time, and mostly because
we were young, and in some cases even cute, it went over OK.

I won't bother you with all our names, since you'll only forget them and anyway there was only one that really mattered. If any of the others play a part along the way I'll name them then.

The one that mattered, matters even, was called Beth and the week before we left she had her hair restyled in a Louise Brooks bob. Actually I thought she looked more like Anna Karina in *Vivre Sa Vie* impersonating Louise Brooks than Brooks herself, if you see what I mean. Either way it's obvious I was smitten. As for the rest of how she looked, well, I'm sorry, but I don't feel inclined to go past her hair. Let memory fall lightly on what follows.

We'd been there, I suppose, for a week, long enough at least to have found some kind of routine. A lot depended on the weather. If it was fine we did well, two hour-long sessions in front of the Beauborg and we were made for the day; we could eat and drink and some of us could even stay at the gypsy's hotel. If it rained things were harder. No one wants to stand and watch buskers in the rain, not even in front of the finest new building in the western world, so the only option was to go down into the Métro.

There were good things about that, the sound you get singing in the tunnels is beautiful, it's a cathedral for drifters, for losers, for *loubards*, for my people, and we sounded like angels down there. The bad side was the cops. Those French cops back then were bastards. Thank our lucky stars we were all white, or almost all, and Yaz was a girl so she was OK, but anytime they'd run out of black kids to persecute they were on our case, moving us on, checking our IDs, threatening us with all kinds of shit. One time, the first time, Don talked back to them. We didn't make that mistake twice. They threw him up against the wall and practically ripped his arm off his shoulder as they searched him for drugs. They had no luck there, of course, as even on a good day our budget didn't stretch any further than plastic bottles of *vin rouge*.

John Williams, 'New Shoes', from *Paris Noir: capital crime fiction*, edited by Maxim Jakubowski

✳ ✳ ✳

*Anyone who, like Jeremy Mercer, beds down for free
at the generous and amazing Shakespeare & Company
bookshop is likely to be well and truly on their uppers.
But old hands at poverty show him there are ways and
means of scrounging a decent meal in Paris.*

We turned left out of the bookstore, crossed rue St. Jacques,
and took rue de la Huchette. The narrow street had once been
among the filthiest in Paris and home to a young Napoléon
Bonaparte when he first arrived in the city. Now it was a garish
tourist ghetto, filled with Greek restaurants that competed for
customers with displays of skewered seafood and the scent of
burning fat. Touts stood in the restaurant doorways, playing
merry with the crowds and shattering cheap porcelain plates at
the feet of the more promising herds.

Shakespeare and Company residents clearly weren't worth
wasting plates over, so we negotiated the street with ease. Emerging
at place St. Michel, we cut past the spouting stone lions, along the
flower shops and trendy bars of rue St. André des Arts, then down
boulevard St. Germain until we arrived at a dismal grey building
on rue Mabillon. Two guards stood slouched at the front door,
but Kurt told me to walk straight in as if I belonged. We climbed
two flights of stairs and came to an enormous cafeteria with row
after row of benches and a long snaking line at the food counter.

This was a student restaurant, one of more than a dozen in
Paris. Subsidized by the government, a full meal cost fifteen
francs here, just two American dollars. Technically, one needed
a student identification card, but the line was full of other
impostors like us: a family with three small children, a couple
with shaved heads and scalp studs, a drunken man with a
variety of stains across his shirtfront and down his pant leg.

In exchange for a colourful meal ticket, one received two
bread rolls, a thick bowl of vegetable soup, a generous slice
of Brie, half a boiled egg with a squib of Dijon mayonnaise as
garnish, a main plate of grilled lamb, sautéed potatoes, and

green beans, a strawberry yogurt and even a slice of honey
sponge cake with sliced almonds for dessert. With each morsel
of food added to my tray, the more inclined I was to agree with
my companion: this was the zenith of the cheap Paris meal.

Jeremy Mercer, *Books, Baguettes and Bedbugs*

✳ ✳ ✳

*The gulf between the dreams that can bring people
to Paris and the misery when those dreams fail is
explored in Sparkle Hayter's short story, 'Deus Ex
Machina: a short story about hope'.*

Going through a rough time in a happy and beautiful place like
Paris puts one's misery in sharp relief. The more luminous and
prosperous Paris looks, the more Shay feels excluded from it. Her
self-pity steadily darkens that winter despite her earnest efforts to
make her dismal state of affairs romantic, invoking the spirits of
great writers forged by poverty and depression. After all, while
Hemingway was poor, he found a moveable feast. Orwell, down
and out in Paris, scratching with bugs from old grey mattresses
in flop hotels, sick from the stench of sulphur burned to try to
keep the insects down, found in it all the brilliance to become
a great writer. Then there was the composer Virgil Thomson,
an intimate of Gertrude Stein and Miss Toklas, who once said,
glibly, that he preferred to be poor in Paris than in America
because 'I'd rather starve in a place with good food'.

Shay tried to be buoyed by that philosophy but now she
wonders is it isn't better to starve in a place with bad food,
where the warm gusts of air and laughter escaping through
restaurant doors on cold winter nights are scented with less
delicious flavours and don't remind her how long it has been
since she's been able to afford even a medium-rare *bavette* in
Béarnaise sauce with *frites* and a glass of beer, under ten euros
in most joints in her neighbourhood. And besides, those who
found inspiration and the seeds of prosperity in hard times were

usually iconoclastic geniuses. She isn't sure any more she has even the spark to genius, that she can justify coming here. It had all been done, hadn't it? Every inch of this city, every quirk of the culture, had been covered long before she arrived, right down to the joys of the classic French *pissoir* which Henry Miller spoke about with such eloquence and affection. Most of them were gone now, the ornately decorated circular tin urinals, little green kiosks, open at the top and bottom so you could see the legs and heads of those using them, exchange a friendly wave or have a neighbourly chat. It would be hard to update that – the new version was an oblong booth made of corrugated fibreglass in dull beige or brown. It cost 40 cents to use it, and you had a limited amount of time in the closed, modular bathroom before it flushed itself with water and cleaning chemicals. She'd heard about someone who'd lingered too long in one and drowned.

During this time, she develops a terror that this is how she'll die, not in a public toilet per se, but in some ironic, comic or embarrassing way, which will stick in people's minds so every-thing she has done before will be blotted out by it. Instead of 'award-winning graduate of the Iowa Writers' Workshop and performance artist Shay Rutherford dies' or even, 'artist of some renown in certain circles dies during performance', she'll be remembered as the woman killed by the cork of the bottle of champagne she was opening to celebrate some long-awaited good news, or run over by a truck full of monkeys bound for the zoo, the driver later revealed to be a long-lost cousin, or by a car full of clowns in civilian clothes on their way to a wedding, or simply remembered as the woman killed while walking down the street by the last *Titanic* survivor who falls out of a window while watering her peacock tulips, and, miraculously, survives yet again thanks to Shay's broken body cushioning her fall.

Aware of her awesome ability to make her fears come true, she gets the idea that she should control her own death by killing herself. At this point, she is without hope, and this plan gives her a certain discipline and purpose. A project. She used to be much better at making her dreams come true – for example, her dream of living one day in Paris brought her to Paris.

Sparkle Hayter, 'Deus ex Machina: a Short Story about Hope',
from *Paris Noir*, edited by Maxim Jakubowski

* * *

The sadness at the heart of the poorer parts of Paris is movingly conveyed in this short passage by Julian Green.

In the boulevard de Clichy I watched an old man standing in the drizzle, working two white rats and two fox terriers who were blinking with weariness. The rats ran up and down the man's arm with extraordinary willingness and a patience bordering on the inexhaustible. The dogs, who wore little Tyrolean hats, sat up and begged as often as they were required to but with that wretched look that comes from being hungry, cold, tired, and aware of appearing ridiculous. Beside me a small boy stood gazing earnestly at the animals. After some minutes he drew a large, battered purse from his pocket and, with a gesture that encapsulated all the good-heartedness of ordinary folk, tossed a few coins into the bowl.

Between Clichy and Pigalle the stalls were being demolished beneath a persistent fine rain. I think that, of all the big cities I have seen, Paris is one of the saddest, notwithstanding the reputation for gaiety it has inherited from a happy era. Ceaselessly, day and night, poverty and sickness prowl the dreary Montmartre streets that in the tourist's eyes glitter like a paradise of carefree pleasure ...

Julian Green, *Paris*, translated by J. A. Underwood

* * *

And now for something more up-beat! When Shusha Guppy arrives from Persia to study at the Sorbonne, every detail of her new life in a new city is vivid and exciting.

Left alone in my new room, I unpacked my suitcase and pushed it under the bed. Tomorrow I would start my French course and perhaps meet some of the students in the Foyer to whom Madame Giroux had suggested introducing me. Meanwhile I sat near the hot water pipe by the window to keep warm and watch the spectacle in the street. This would become my favourite spot – warm in winter and cool in summer, when the window was open.

Being a short, cross street, rue des Bénédictines did not have much traffic, but there were some regular features. Once a week the rag-and-bone man came, pushing his overloaded wheelbarrow while shouting incomprehensible words. No one ever sold to or bought anything from him, nor did he seem particularly interested: he was like a clockwork toy, wound up to go through the motions and stopping when the spring ran down. Less regularly we had visits from the Street-Singer, a large inebriated woman accompanied by a tiny man who held her arm when they walked, and who stepped aside to become her audience while she sang, looking at her in rapt silence. You could hear her nanny-goat tremolo and rolling Rs as soon as she turned into the street – shades of Edith Piaf, whose songs she sang, and on whose legendary popularity as a street-singer she relied for sympathy and generosity. When she reached the middle of the road underneath my window, she would stop and bellow: '*Quand il me prrrrend dans ses brrrras, qu'il me parrrrle tout bas, je vois la vie en ro-o-o-ose.*' When the song was over, she would shout 'thank you, ladies and gentlemen, thank you.' Windows would open and coins would start showering down, not very many, but enough for the singer's companion to rush around picking them up and putting them in a beret. Then he would take the Diva's arm and move on as she started another song, her tremolo fading as she disappeared round the corner. [...]

On the corner of the street was our local café – dark, drab and frequented mostly by workmen, as students and younger people preferred the larger, more cheerful and brightly lit cafés on the boulevards. Its middle-aged owner was surly and taciturn and wore a permanent scowl. His plump blonde wife, who ran the place with him, was shrilly garrulous, and together they made up a kind of Punch-and-Judy show without the blows. They opened early in the morning, when their first clients stopped at the counter for a quick espresso, or a glass of *fine*, on their way to work, and stayed open till after midnight. They could not have had more than five hours' sleep a night, six nights a week, and unlike the Grocers they did not have the energy of youth. No wonder he was bad-tempered and she so shrill. Who wouldn't be? [...]

When you turned the corner of our relatively quiet street the scene changed: rue Saint-Jacques, one of the long arteries of the Latin Quarter which climbed uphill from the embankment towards Montparnasse, was particularly busy at our level. Crowds of students hurried along the narrow pavements to and from the Sorbonne some five hundred yards away, cars rushed by hooting and braking to avoid unwary pedestrians spilling over onto the cobblestoned road, bicycles weaved their way through the traffic.

In the middle of the block was Saint Benedict's church, a modest eighteenth-century edifice, its façade blackened by time, which on Sundays rang its bells and opened its heavy doors to receive a varied crowd of worshippers: middle-aged couples with their children dressed in their Sunday best, clutching their missals in their gloved hands, elderly women in old-fashioned hats holding the arms of their equally ancient husbands, a few students. During the week the front door of the church was closed and you only saw one or two 'regulars' go in at odd times of the day through the little side entrance, sallow-skinned, doleful-eyed, inward-looking lone pilgrims, mostly women, in need of prayer or confession. A smell of incense and wax pervaded the cold air. Light filtered through stained-glass rosettes between the arches, relieving the obscurity, while a few elongated candles burned quietly beneath a statue of the Virgin in a niche creating a pool of moonlight around her feet. Saint Benedict's contained no famous works of art, but it had paintings of the Stations of the Cross along the left wall and ornamental candlesticks and vessels displayed on a table under the Crucifix. It was the first church I had visited. How different from the bareness of our local mosque at home! Even the grand mosques of Isfahan and Shiraz, with their sumptuously coloured tiles and architectural harmony, were empty inside, save for the rough mats on the floor – nothing must distract from the concentration on prayer. Here images and ornaments created an atmosphere conducive to spiritual communion. Two different approaches to the same goal. I often stopped on my way home for a few minutes of quiet reflection.

Shusha Guppy, *A Girl in Paris*

* * *

It isn't only young people from all over the world who have brought their 'high hopes' of life to Paris: the city's own sons and daughters, too, have pursued their dreams and ambitions in her familiar streets ... and libraries. Here's novelist, philosopher and feminist Simone de Beauvoir recalling the feelings of elation and energy attending the start of her dreams ...

The beginning of this academic year was unlike any other. By deciding to enter for the competition, I had at last escaped from the labyrinth in which I had been going round in circles for the last three years: I was now on my way to the future. From now on, every day had its meaning: it was taking me further on my road to final liberation. I was spurred on by the difficulty of the enterprise: there was no longer any question of straying from the straight and narrow path, or of becoming bored. Now that I had something definite to work for, I found that the earth could give me all I wanted; I was released from disquiet, despair, and from all my regrets. 'In this diary, I shall no longer make note of tragic self-communings, but only of the events of every day.' I had the feeling that after a painful apprenticeship my real life was just beginning, and I threw myself into it gladly.

In October, while the Sorbonne was closed, I spent my days in the Bibliothèque Nationale. I had obtained permission to have my lunch out: I would buy bread and rillette and eat them in the gardens of the Palais Royal while watching the petals of the late roses fall; sitting on the benches, navvies would be munching thick sandwiches and drinking cheap red wine. If it was raining, I would take shelter in the Café Biard with bricklayers eating out of mess-tins; I was delighted to escape from the ritual of family meals; by reducing food to its essential elements I felt I was taking another step in the direction of freedom. I would go back to the library; I was studying the theory of relativity, and was passionately interested in it. From time to time I would look up at the other readers and lean back proudly in my armchair: among these specialists, scholars, researchers, and thinkers I felt at home. I no longer felt myself to be rejected by my environment; it was I who had rejected it in order to enter that society – of which I saw here a cross-section – in which all those minds that are interested in finding out the truth communicate with each other across the distances of space and time. I, too, was taking part in the effort which humanity makes to know, to understand, to express itself: I was engaged in a great collective enterprise which would release me for ever from the bonds of loneliness. What a victory! I would settle down to work again. At a quarter to six, the superintendent's voice would solemnly announce: 'Gentlemen – we shall – very soon – be – closing.' It was always a surprise, after leaving my studies, to come back to the shops outside, the lights, the passers-by, and the dwarf who sold bunches of violets near the Théâtre Français. I would walk slowly, giving myself up to the melancholy of evening and of my return home.

Simone de Beauvoir, *Memoirs of a Dutiful Daughter*

✻ ✻ ✻

Lost Illusions *is one of the most famous novels by the exhaustingly prolific Honoré de Balzac (1799–1850). A young man from the provinces tries to make his way in*

*Parisian society and recognizes, early on, the gap between
the life he knows and the life of the sophisticated capital.*

In the course of his first random stroll through the boulevards and
the rue de la Paix, Lucien, like all new-comers to Paris, took more
stock of things than of persons. In Paris, it is first of all the general
pattern that commands attention. The luxury of the shops, the
height of the buildings, the busy to-and-fro of carriages, the ever-
present contrast between extreme luxury and extreme indigence,
all these things are particularly striking. Abashed at the sight of
this alien crowd, the imaginative young man felt as if he himself
was enormously diminished. People who in the provinces enjoy a
certain amount of consideration and at every step they take meet
with some proof of their own importance can in no wise accustom
themselves to this sudden and total devaluation. Some transition is
needed between the two states of being a somebody at home and a
nobody in Paris; and those who pass too abruptly from one to the
other experience a feeling of annihilation. For a young poet used to
having a sounding-board for all his feelings, an ear into which he
could pour all his thoughts and a kindred soul to share his slightest
impressions, Paris was to prove a fearsome desert. Lucien had not
gone to fetch his fine blue coat, so that he felt embarrassed by the
sorry, not to say ruinous, condition of his clothes as he was returning
to Madame de Bargeton's flat at a time when he deemed she would
be back. The Baron du Châtelet was already there, and he took
them both out to dine at the Rocher-de-Cancale. Lucien, stunned
by the rapid whirl of life in Paris, could say nothing to Louise, as all
three of them were together inside the carriage. But he squeezed her
hand, and she gave a friendly response to all the thoughts he was
thus expressing. After dinner Châtelet took his two guests to the
Vaudeville Theatre. Lucien felt secretly displeased to see du Châtelet
and was cursing the ill-luck which had brought him to Paris. The
Director of Taxes alleged his own ambition as an excuse for his
arrival there: he was hoping to be appointed Secretary-General in
a civil service department and to enter the Council of State as a

master of requests; he had come to ask that the promises made to him should be honoured, for a man like himself could not remain a mere Director of Taxes; he would prefer to be nothing at all, become a deputy or return to a diplomatic career. He was puffing himself out, and Lucien vaguely recognized in the elderly fop the advantage which a man of the world enjoys in Parisian society; but above all he was ashamed to owe any enjoyment to him. Whereas the poet was anxious and ill at ease, the former Secretary to an Imperial Highness was altogether in his element. Just as old sea-dogs mock at greenhorn sailors who have not found their sea-legs, so du Châtelet smiled at his rival's hesitancy, his wonderment, the questions he asked and the little blunders he made through inexperience. But the pleasure which Lucien felt at his first visit to a theatre in Paris compensated for the annoyance which his blunders caused him. It was a memorable evening for him, thanks to the unvoiced repudiation of a great number of his ideas about life in the provinces. His little world was broadening out and society was assuming vaster proportions. The proximity of several beautiful Parisian women, so elegantly and so daintily attired, made him aware that Madame de Bargeton's *toilette*, though passably ambitious, was behind the times: neither the material nor the way it was cut, nor the colours were in fashion. The hair-style he had found so seductive in Angoulême struck him as being in deplorable taste compared with the delicate inventiveness which lent distinction to the other women present. 'Will she remain like that?' he wondered, not knowing that she had spent the day preparing a transformation. In the provinces no occasion arises for choice or comparison: one sees the same physiognomies day by day and confers a conventional beauty on them. Once she has moved to Paris a woman accepted as pretty in the provinces commands not the slightest attention, for she is beautiful only by virtue of the proverb: 'In a community of the blind, one-eyed people reign supreme.'

Honoré de Balzac, *Lost Illusions*, translated by Herbert J. Hunt

* * *

*Like Balzac's Lucien, Englishman Michael Sadler
decides to escape the provincial life of a British village
and head for Paris ... though in a more light-hearted
spirit. And it isn't hard to see why the City of Light
should prove an irresistible temptation.*

What exactly was I doing this hot Saturday on the Rouen-Paris motorway in my red Mazda with its unpasteurized flashing light?

For a long time I had been secretly troubled by the idea that I wanted to live in France. First there was the language. I'd had a French mistress at primary school – she was married to a local businessman – and a French master at secondary. I was in love with the first and in awe of the second. When they spoke French, they were different, exciting, electric. I'd always wondered who I might be if I could speak it. Then there was the country. I suffered from a kind of nostalgia for something I'd never known. This sneaking feeling was exacerbated when the rain formed a puddle in the tarpaulin over the pond at the bottom of the garden, when moss crept like athlete's foot between the carrots, when the bread tasted of pap, and the baker's was empty at four. I occasionally dreamed of packing a suitcase and heading for Dieppe. At least I'd arrive in time to buy a loaf.

Then, one day, a letter arrived on the mat offering me a year's sabbatical leave in France. [...]

Thanks to membership of the EU everything was easy to arrange: I filled in form E–128 in case I was ill – you pay the doctor, get him to sign it, send it off to Newcastle and wait twelve years to be reimbursed; paid the 400 per cent supplement on the car insurance which protects you from the record death-toll on French roads, had a flick through the succinct twenty-five-page instruction booklet on how to obtain a *carte de séjour* and *Robert est votre oncle*.

I would have liked to slip away without any fuss but the village was determined not to let me *filer à l'anglaise* (take French leave). We had to have a 'French party'. 'Come dressed as a frog!' stipulated the invitation delicately. Abesbury under Lyme, the desirable village where I rented a refurbished workman's cottage, was unaccustomed to this kind of excitement. It regularly won prizes – for lawns, floral displays, even for its tip: a tasteful marriage of green bins and hornbeam. Above all it deserved an Emmy for *ennui*. Nothing ever happened. The fire brigade were only ever called out to rescue cats with vertigo on the oak on the green, and the nearest we ever came to danger was the purchase of a Sunday joint to prove that we were ready to die of BSE for the country. There was a rumour that the vicar was on Ecstasy but it turned out to be high blood pressure. […]

The party was announced for seven. The guests began to arrive at five to.

Anthony Brick, the interior decorator, confected a *képi* out of a cornflakes packet and came as General de Gaulle. Harold Holms came as a member of the French Resistance wearing the collar of his wife's trenchcoat turned up. As the mac was too small and buttoned tight he was very red in the face and looked more like Boris Yeltsin. Peter Blake wore the classic striped breton pullover complete with a string of onions – which turned out to be real, smelly and uncomfortable for his dancing partners. Maurice Hope, an insurance agent who had a topiary head of Margaret Thatcher at the entrance to his thatched cottage, had made himself a red *légion d'honneur* for his buttonhole. We spent the evening pulling on it like a door bell and going rrrrriiiinnngggg. Brian Topps was very brown after his holiday on the Costa Brava and had found himself a rasta wig. He was supposed to be the tennis star Yannick Noah but no one had heard of Yannick Noah and everyone thought he was a mop. Robert Scott, fat and full of himself, was wearing a false nose. Everybody called him '*mon général*' and saluted, which made him angry as he believed he was the spitting image of Gérard Depardieu.

The most surprising were the ladies. Anyone driving by accident through Abesbury that Saturday evening wouldn't have believed his eyes. The main street – which stretched from the surviving sub-post office to St John's Church, passing by the seed merchants and the souvenir shop – looked like Pigalle on a hot summer night. Extraordinary creatures, encased in tight satin, their breasts welling up and out of their laced bodices like cream boiling over from a saucepan, waited on the pavements under the lampposts as their husbands parked the Rover. [...]

At midnight we all joined the gnomes in the garden to sing 'Alouette' and 'Frère Jacques'. Glasses of sparkling Bulgarian chardonnay were raised in my honour. My pockets were full of addresses in case of need – including a guaranteed supply of Marmite and Worcester Sauce in the Dordogne some 500 kilometres south of Paris. High spot of the closing ceremony – I was presented with a copy of *A Year in Provence* signed by the whole village. The book was given to me in a box which also contained a pair of Union Jack braces. The injunction to keep the flag flying greatly amused the nudge-nudge contingent. As we took leave, kissing each other at least six times on each cheek in what was supposed to be a French manner, the village resounded to cries of '*Au revoir*', '*Bonne chance*' and even a surprising '*Vive la France!*' This triggered off an immediate response from the drunk Bob Scott who sang 'God Save the Queen' in the spectral orange light of the lamppost on to which he was hanging.

Such was France as viewed from the cliffs of Abesbury under Lyme.

The next morning, as I drove out of the sleepy village, the curtains were still closed. It was a sign. England had been my pillow.

La France serait mon réveil.

Michael Sadler, *An Englishman in Paris*

✳ ✳ ✳

*It isn't only individuals who manifest their high hopes
of life in Paris. The French nation itself seems to express
its great ambitions for itself through the very delinea-
tions of its capital and the national events staged there.
Travel writer Jan Morris finds herself unexpectedly
caught up in the mood on the Champs-Élysées.*

More insidiously seductive, I think, is the glory of France, perhaps
because it has always struck me as being perfectly humourless.
One cannot laugh at the swank and strut of it, just as it would
have seemed unkind to snigger at the gaunt solemnity of General
de Gaulle, to whom all life seemed so tragically in earnest, and
to whom the idea of France not being a Power would have
been preposterous. I was in Paris once when for festive reasons
the Champs-Élysées was cleared of all traffic, allowing pedestrians to stroll the length of it from the Place de la Concorde
to L'Étoile. I undertook the walk churlishly, for I have always
disliked the pomp and monotony of Haussmann's boulevards.
As I walked the gentle slope of the great street, however, through
the green parks, past the line of rich buildings, towards the Arc
de Triomphe revealing itself at the end of it – as I strode up there
along the very centre of the avenue, with thousands of Parisians
in high proud spirits all around me, minute by minute I found
myself falling into a genuine Sun King or Gaullist swagger. One
can never be indifferent to France, Alexis de Tocqueville said. It
was the most brilliant and dangerous country in Europe, he said.
Besides, to my mind French glory is true glory.

Jan Morris, *Europe: an intimate journey*

* * *

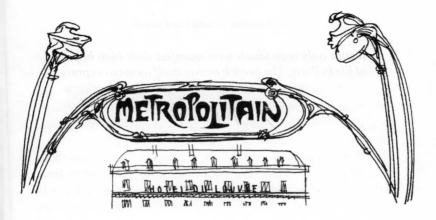

Location, location ...

Lovers of Joanne Harris's Chocolat *as well as of Paris will be delighted with them being brought together in* The Lollipop Shoes *in which Vianne brings her children to Paris, starting a new life in one of the capital's iconic locations: Montmartre.*

Montmartre is a village, so my mother used to say; an island rising out of the Paris fog. It's not like Lansquenet, of course, but even so, it's a good place, with a little flat above the shop and a kitchen at back, and a room for Rosette and one for Anouk, under the eaves with the birds' nests.

Our *chocolaterie* was once a tiny café, run by a lady called Marie-Louise Poussin, who lived up on the first floor. Madame had lived here for twenty years; had seen the death of her husband and son, and, now, in her sixties and in failing health, still stubbornly refused to retire. She needed help; I needed a job. I agreed to run her business for a small salary and the use of the rooms on the second floor, and as Madame grew less able to cope, we changed the shop to a *chocolaterie*.

I ordered stock, managed accounts, organized deliveries, handled sales. I dealt with repairs and building work. Our arrangement has lasted for over three years, and we have become accustomed to it. We don't have a garden, or very much space, but we can see the Sacré-Coeur from our window, rising above the streets like an airship. Anouk has started secondary school – the Lycée Jules Renard, just off the Boulevard des Batignolles – and she's bright, and works hard; I'm proud of her.

Rosette is almost four years old, although, of course, she does not go to school. Instead she stays in the shop with me, making patterns on the floor with buttons and sweets, arranging them in rows according to colour and shape, or filling page after page in her drawing-books with little pictures of animals. She is learning sign language, and is fast acquiring vocabulary, including the signs for *good, more, come, here, see, boat, yum, picture, again, monkey, ducks* and most recently – and to Anouk's delight – *bullshit.*

And when we close the shop for lunch, we go to the Parc de la Turlure, where Rosette likes to feed the birds, or a little further to Montmartre cemetery, which Anouk loves for its gloomy magnificence and its many cats. Or I talk to the other shop owners in the *quartier*: to Lauren Pinson, who run the grubby little *café-bar* across the square; to his customers, regulars for the most part, who come for breakfast and stay till noon; to Madame Pinot, who sells postcards and religious bric-a-brac on the corner; to the artists who camp out on the Place du Tertre hoping to attract the tourists there.

There is a clear distinction here between the inhabitants of the Butte and the rest of Montmartre. The Butte is superior in every respect – at least, to my neighbours of the Place des Faux-Monnayeurs – a last outpost of Parisian authenticity in a city now overrun with foreigners.

These people never buy chocolates. The rules are strict, though unwritten. Some places are for outsiders only; like the *boulangerie-pâtisserie* on the Place de la Galette, with its art deco mirrors and coloured glass and baroque piles of macaroons. Locals go to Rue des Trois Frères, to the cheaper, plainer *boulangerie*, where the bread is better and the croissants are baked fresh every day. In the same way, locals eat at Le P'tit Pinson, all vinyl-topped tables and *plat du jour*, whereas outsiders like ourselves secretly prefer La Bohème, or even worse, La Maison Rose, which no true son or daughter of the Butte would ever frequent, any more than they would pose for an artist at the terrace of a café on the Place du Tertre, or go to Mass at the Sacré-Coeur.

Joanne Harris, *The Lollipop Shoes*

✻ ✻ ✻

The difference between being an 'outsider' and an 'insider' to a neighbourhood in Paris is picked up also by T. E. Carhart: it is his involvement with the local piano workshop that finally turns him into an accepted member of the local community.

Our *quartier* is in a quiet part of the *Rive Gauche*, and its atmosphere is in many ways less frenetic than other parts of Paris. The Seine divides the city into roughly equal halves, north and south, and as you float down the river from east to west, the southern half is on your left: the Left Bank. This part of the city retains a quiet air, one less infused with commerce than with narrow residential streets, numerous parks, and several of the urban campuses of the University of Paris. Although much of it has been gentrified and real student poverty is as distant as Puccini's *La Bohème*, artists and artisans, craftsmen and skilled labourers still can be found in many of the neighborhoods. The building we converted into our apartment had been a carpentry shop in the nineteenth century, and its high ceilings and multiple skylights suited my wife's work as a photographer. Luc's atelier [the 'piano workshop' of the title] was hidden, but as I came to know the neighborhood better I realized that it wasn't really surprising that his activities should find a home in this *quartier*. The avenues with their cafés and plane trees look like much of the rest of Paris, but along the side streets the courtyards hold secrets that aren't readily found elsewhere.

Although I didn't fully realize it at the time, Luc's invitation to continue to stop by the atelier changed the face of the neighbourhood for me. I was now a 'client', a member of the loose assemblage of neighbors, friends, and customers whose paths sometimes crossed in the secluded back room of his shop. It was like being asked to join a club where neither democracy nor personal influence prevailed; pianos were the thing and only Luc could let you in. We had lived nearby for almost three years, getting to know neighbors, shopkeepers, and tradesmen in the daily routine of running a household, but this was my first experience of a real *vie de quartier* from the inside, a neighborhood life that was richer and more varied than anything I had imagined.

T. E. Carhart, *The Piano Shop on the Left Bank*

✻ ✻ ✻

One of the unmissable places of pilgrimage for the more bookish visitor to Paris is undoubtedly 'Shakespeare & Company', founded and, at the time of writing, still run by a redoubtable and visionary American, George Whitman (though now with the assistance of his daughter). Bookshop, free hotel and library for penniless writers, venue for literary readings, and major tourist attraction, it has attained mythological status and is really worth a visit. One Canadian writer who found sanctuary there, Jeremy Mercer, records his experiences in Books, Baguettes and Bedbugs. *Here he gives the story behind 'Shakespeare & Company'.*

For the better part of a century, an English bookstore by the name of Shakespeare and Company has served as a haven for artists, writers, and other wayward souls of Paris.

It began with Sylvia Beach. Born in Baltimore and raised in New Jersey at the end of the nineteenth century, Beach was fourteen years old when she first travelled to Europe. Her father, a Presbyterian minister, had been appointed the assistant to the pastor of the American Church in Paris and moved his family to France in 1901. Beach tumbled into love with the city, and after working as a nurse in World War I, she returned to make Paris her home. Always of a literary mind and keenly aware of the need for English books, she opened the original Shakespeare and Company in November 1919 on rue Dupuytren. In 1922, Beach moved her store to rue de l'Odéon, a side street in the sixth arrondissement, near St.-Germain-des-Prés.

This strange nook of a bookstore became the hub for a generation of American and British writers in Paris. The likes of F. Scott Fitzgerald, Gertrude Stein, and Ezra Pound gathered here to borrow books, discuss literary matters, and drink hot tea in the private parlor at the back of the store. [...] Most notably, it was Beach who raised the money to edit and publish her friend James Joyce's manuscript *Ulysses* when other publishers rejected it as scandalous and sexually provocative.

"There was a tremendous amount of talent in Paris then," Beach wrote later, "and my shop seemed to be a gathering place for most of it."

The original Shakespeare and Company was shut down in 1941 when the Nazis occupied Paris. Romantics say the store was closed when Beach refused to sell her last copy of *Finnegan's Wake* to a Nazi officer, while others claim the shop's reputation for creative nonconformity worried the Germans. Whatever the case, Shakespeare and Company was closed for the duration of the occupation and Beach spent World War II in an internment camp. Hemingway himself liberated the premises when he entered Paris with the American troops in 1944, but Beach preferred to retire. She never opened the shop doors again.

A decade later, a similar bookstore opened on the Left Bank, not far from the old shop on the rue de l'Odéon. It, too, was run by a rogue American, this time a vagabond dreamer and writer by the name of George Whitman. He'd spent years wandering the world, and after settling in Paris in the 1940s, he devoted his life to the quixotic pursuit of bookseller. [...]

Shakespeare and Company sits on the very left edge of the Left Bank. The store is close enough to the Seine that when one is standing in the front doorway, a well-thrown apple core will easily reach river water. From this same doorway, there is an inspired view of the Île de la Cité and one can contemplate the cathedral of Notre Dame, the Hôtel Dieu hospital, and the imposing block of the main police prefecture.

The bookstore's actual address is 37 rue de la Bûcherie. It's an odd cobbled street that begins at rue St. Jacques, runs for one block, hits the public park of St.-Julien-le-Pauvre, then continues on for another two blocks before ending at the square Restif-de-la-Bretonne. The bookstore is on the part of the rue de la Bûcherie close to rue St. Jacques, where, thanks to a quirk of city planning, there are only buildings on the south side of the street, which is what gives the bookstore its splendid view.

This end of the street is reserved for pedestrians, but this is only part of the reason it retains a certain calm. There is also a tiny city garden that separates the bookstore from the racing traffic of Quai de Montebello and then the sidewalk widens in front of 37 rue de la Bûcherie to create an almost private esplanade for Shakespeare and Company. For the coup de grâce, there are two young cherry trees on this esplanade and a green Wallace drinking fountain sitting majestically to the side. All this gives the bookstore an air of tranquillity that is shocking in the midst of the frenzy and noise of downtown Paris.

As for the bookstore itself, there are actually two entrances. Facing the shop, the main part of the store with the narrow green door I entered on the day of the tea party is on the right. It is here that one finds the famous yellow-and-green wooden Shakespeare and Company sign and the broad picture window. To the left of the main store, there is a second, smaller storefront. This is the antiquarian room. Along with the shelves of centuries-old books, the antiquarian room has a desk, a lovely stuffed armchair, and, of course, a creaky but thoroughly sleepable bed.

When I arrived after my coffee with Fernanda, it was nearing dark and the streetlights were flickering to life around me. The window of the main shop glowed a soft yellow against the early night, and at the desk there was an elderly man with a rumpled suit and a faraway look in his eyes. From the photographs I'd seen the day before, I knew this man to be George. Taking one last breath for courage, I stepped inside.

Jeremy Mercer, *Books, Baguettes & Bedbugs*

❋ ❋ ❋

Around the corner from Shakespeare & Company, visitors enjoying the little side-roads off the rue Saint-Jacques and marvelling at the Val de Grâce church will be sharing the same pleasures as T. E. Carhart.

I walked home from a friend's apartment in the Latin Quarter by a roundabout way, purposely taking the narrow street that leads past my favourite church in Paris, Val de Grâce. It lies on the rue Saint Jacques, a small but noisy thoroughfare that has led south since the time when Paris was the Roman city of Lutetia. Its current name derives from its use as a route in the Middle Ages for pilgrims heading to Santiago di Compostela in Spain; or, in the usage the French prefer, *Saint Jacques de Compostelle*. Val de Grâce is a large late Renaissance church that is unusual for Paris; its exuberant carvings and animated façade are more typical of Rome, and the most beautiful dome in the city graces its undulating mass of light yellow stone.

I love walking down the cramped and busy sidewalks of Saint Jacques, suddenly to come upon an unexpected widening of the street and the glory of this Renaissance pile set back behind gold-tipped iron pickets. This, too, is more like Rome than the Paris of Haussmann's broad boulevards and triumphal esplanades. It's extravagant, voluptuous and very grand, and yet its setting is strangely intimate.

T. E. Carhart, *The Piano Shop on the Left Bank*

✱ ✱ ✱

Haussmann's broad boulevards changed the face of Paris utterly. One of the results of 'Haussmannization' was the disappearance of many of the old 'arcades' which had been such a feature of the city. There are still a few left, but fewer than there used to be. Two very famous texts about the old arcades of Paris are the magisterial collection of notes by the philosopher and writer Walter Benjamin (1892–1940), and the first half of Louis Aragon's Paris Peasant. *Benjamin relates how, at the end of 1919, the Surrealists, Aragon and Breton, disliking Montparnasse and Montmartre, transferred their regular meetings with friends to a café in the Passage de l'Opéra and that Aragon devoted 135 pages to this arcade (in* Paris Peasant). *Unfortunately, construction of the Boulevard Haussmann led to the arcade's destruction. But at least it is preserved in the aspic of Benjamin's and Aragon's words. Here's a fragment from Aragon, saying something general about the arcades and leading us to the very entrance of the Passage de l'Opéra.*

How oddly this light suffuses the covered arcades which abound in Paris in the vicinity of the main boulevards and which are rather disturbingly named *passages*, as though no one had the right to linger for more than an instant in those sunless corridors. A glaucous gleam, seemingly filtered through deep water, with the special quality of pale brilliance of a leg suddenly revealed under a lifted skirt. The great American passion for city planning, imported into Paris by a prefect of police during the Second Empire and now being applied to the task of redrawing the map of our capital in straight lines, will soon spell the doom of these human aquariums. Although the life that originally quickened them has drained away, they deserve, nevertheless, to be regarded as the secret repositories of several modern myths: it is only today, when the pickaxe menaces them, that they have at last become the true sanctuaries of a cult of the ephemeral, the ghostly landscape of damnable pleasures and professions. Places that were incomprehensible yesterday, and that tomorrow will never know.

'Today, the Boulevard Haussmann has reached the Rue Lafitte,' remarked *L'Intransigeant* the other day. A few more paces forward by this giant rodent and, after it has devoured the block of houses separating it from the Rue Le Peletier, it will inexorably gash open the thicket whose twin arcades run through the Passage de l'Opéra, before finally emerging diagonally on to the Boulevard des Italiens. It will unite itself to that broad avenue somewhere near where the Café Louis XVI now stands, with a singular kind of kiss whose cumulative effect on the vast body of Paris is quite unpredictable. It seems possible, though, that a good part of the human river which carries incredible floods of dreamers and dawdlers from the Bastille to the Madeleine may divert itself through this new channel, and thus modify the ways of thought of a whole district, perhaps of a whole world. We are doubtless about to witness a complete upheaval of the established fashions in casual strolling and prostitution, and it may well be that this thoroughfare, which is bound to make the boulevards and the Quartier Saint-Lazare far more easily accessible to each other, will see entirely new types of person saunter along its pavements, hitherto unknown specimens whose whole life will hesitate between the two zones of attraction in which they are equally involved, and who will be the chief protagonists of tomorrow's mysteries.

Future mysteries will arise from the ruins of today's. Let us take a stroll along this Passage de l'Opéra, and have a closer look at it …

Louis Aragon, *Paris Peasant*, translated by Simon Watson Taylor

* * *

The Lycée Condorcet has long been recognised as probably the best school in Paris, its famous past pupils being

too many to list but including poet Paul Verlaine, novelist Marcel Proust, artist Toulouse-Lautrec, singer-songwriter Serge Gainsbourg, and the extraordinary writer/artist/ film-maker and general man-about-town Jean Cocteau. His famous novel, Les Enfants Terribles, *begins with pupils from the school being 'let out' at the end of the school day into a Paris thick with snow. Schoolboys plus snow equals snowball fight, of course – the most famous one in literature. For anyone in the know about the school's location on the rue du Havre, Cocteau's reference to its address as being rue d'Amsterdam and being called 'small' is accounted for by the fact that an annexe of the school was opened nearby in the rue du Havre. (And the French 'reverse' numbering system for school years means their 'fifth years' are much younger than ours.)*

That portion of old Paris known as the Cité Monthiers is bounded on the one side by the rue de Clichy, on the other by the rue d'Amsterdam. Should you choose to approach it from the rue de Clichy, you would come to a pair of wrought iron gates: but if you were to come by way of the rue d'Amsterdam, you would reach another entrance, open day and night, and giving access to a block of tenements, and then to the courtyard proper, an oblong court containing a row of small private dwellings secretively disposed beneath the flat towering walls of the main structure. Clearly these little houses must be the abode of artists. The windows are blind, covered with photographers' drapes, but it is comparatively easy to guess what they conceal: rooms chock-a-block with weapons and lengths of brocade, with canvases depicting basketfuls of cats, or the families of Bolivian diplomats. Here dwells the Master, illustrious, unacknowledged, well-nigh prostrated by the weight of his public honours and commissions, with all this dumb provincial stronghold to seal him from disturbance.

Twice a day, however, at half past ten in the morning and four o'clock in the afternoon, the silence is shattered by the sound of tumult. The doors of the little Lycée Condorcet, opposite number 72b rue d'Amsterdam, open, and a horde of schoolboys emerges to occupy the Cité and set up their head-quarters. Thus it has re-assumed a sort of medieval character – something in the nature of a Court of Love, a Wonder Fair, an Athletes' Stadium, a Stamp Exchange; also a gangsters' tribune cum place of public execution; also a breeding ground for rags – rags to be hatched out finally in class, after long incubation, before the incredulous eyes of the authorities. Terrors they are, these lads, and no mistake – the terrors of the Fifth. […]

There was snow that evening. The snow had gone on falling steadily since yesterday, thereby radically altering the original design. The Cité had withdrawn in Time; the snow seemed no longer to be impartially distributed over the whole warm living earth, but to be dropping, piling only upon this one isolated spot.

The hard muddy ground had already been smashed, churned up, crushed, stamped into slides by children on their way to school. The soiled snow made ruts along the gutter. But the snow had also become the snow on porches, steps, and house-fronts: feather-weight packages, mats, cornices, odds and ends of wadding, ethe-real yet crystallized, seemed, instead of blurring the outlines of the stone, to quicken it, to imbue it with a kind of presage.

Gleaming with the soft effulgence of a luminous dial, the snow's incandescence, self-engendered, reached inward to probe the very soul of luxury and draw it forth through stone till it was visible, till it was that fabric magically upholstering the Cité, shrinking it and transforming it into a phantom drawing-room.

Seen from below, the prospect had less to recommend it. The street lamps shed a feeble light upon what looked like a deserted battle-field. Frost-flayed, the ground had split, was broken up into fissured blocks, like crazy pavement. In front of every gully-hole, a stack of grimy snow stood ominous, a potential ambush; the gas-jets flickered in a villainous north-easter; and the dark holes and corners already hid their dead.

Viewed from this angle, the illusion produced was altogether

103

different. Houses were no longer boxes in some legendary theatre but houses deliberately blacked out, barricaded by their occupants to hinder the enemy's advance. In fact the entire Cité had lost its civil status, its character of open mart, fair-ground, and place of execution. The blizzard had commandeered it totally, imposed upon it a specifically military role, a particular strategic function. By ten minutes past four, the operation had developed to the point where none could venture from the porch without incurring risk. Beneath that porch the reservists were assembled, their numbers swollen by the newcomers who continued to arrive singly or two by two.

'Seen Dargelos?'

'Yes ... No ... I don't know.'

This reply came from one of two youths engaged in bringing in one of the first casualties. He had a handkerchief tied round his knee and was hopping along between them and clinging to their shoulders.

Jean Cocteau, *Les Enfants Terribles*, translated by Rosamund Lehmann

✳ ✳ ✳

It's hard to imagine Paris without the Eiffel Tower – and to imagine how frightening it must have been for those of a more nervous disposition to ascend this unbelievable structure when it was first built for the Universal Exhibition in 1889, celebrating the centenary of the French Revolution. In Murder on the Eiffel Tower, *Claude Izner recreates the trepidation of a harassed middle-aged woman who has been persuaded to take her sister's children to the Exhibition and to ascend the Tower. But it isn't the Tower she needs to fear ...*

Pointing straight up into the sky on the other side of the Seine, Gustave Eiffel's bronze-coloured tower was reminiscent of a giant streetlamp topped with gold. Panic-stricken, Eugénie searched for a pretext to get out of climbing it. When she couldn't think of one, she laid a hand on her pounding heart. *If I survive this I shall say fifty Paternosters at Notre-Dame d'Auteuil.*

The bus drew up in front of the enormous Trocadero palace, flanked by minarets. Down below, beyond the grey ribbon of the river filled with boats, the fifty hectares of the Universal Exposition were spread before them.

Tightly clutching her bag, her eyes fixed on the children, Eugénie began her descent into hell. She charged down Colline de Chaillot, passing the fruits of the world display, the tortured bonsai of the Japanese garden, and the dark entrance to 'Journey to the Centre of the Earth' without a second glance. Though the whalebones of her corset chafed her ribs and her feet begged for mercy, she did not slacken her pace. She just wanted to get this over and done with as soon as possible and get back on terra firma ...

Finally, she held out her tickets and pushed the children under the canopy of the Pont d'Iéna. 'Listen to me carefully,' she said slowly and deliberately. 'If you stray from me by so much as a centimetre – do you hear me? a centimetre – we're going home.'

Then she plunged headlong into the fray. A huge crowd was jostling around the multicoloured kiosks, forming a human tide of French people and foreigners of all races. The minstrels of Leicester Square, with their soot-blackened faces, led the way along the left bank, to the rhythm of banjos.

With pounding heart, and overwhelmed by the noise, Eugénie clung to Gontran, who was unmoved by the hubbub. The Exposition seemed to come at them from all sides. Jostled between the street vendors, the Annamese rickshaw-pullers and Egyptian donkey-drivers, they finally succeeded in joining the queue in front of the southern pillar of the Tower.

Moving reluctantly along in the queue, Eugénie looked enviously at the elegant young people comfortably installed in special rolling chairs, pushed by employees in peak caps. *That's what I need ...*

'Aunt, look!'

She looked up and saw a forest of crossbars and small beams, in the midst of which a lift slid up and down. At once she was seized with a desire to flee as fast and as far as her exhausted legs would carry her.

She dimly heard Gontran's monotonous voice: 'Three hundred and one metres … leading straight up to the second floor … four lifts. Otis, Combaluzier … '

Otis, Combaluzier. Something about those strange names suddenly reminded her of the projectile vehicle, in that book by Jules Verne whose title escaped her.

'Those preferring to walk up the one thousand seven hundred and ten steps will take an hour to do so … '

She remembered now: it was *From the Earth to the Moon*! What if the cables snapped … ?

'Aunt, I want a balloon! A helium balloon! A blue one! Give me a sou, Aunt, a sou!'

A clout on the ear more like!

She regained her self-control. A poor relation, given a roof over her head out of pure charity, could not afford to give free rein to her feelings. Regretfully she held out a sou to Hector.

Gontran was still reciting impassively from the Exhibition Guide. ' … on average, eleven thousand visitors a day, and the Tower can accommodate ten thousand people at any one time … '

He stopped abruptly, sensing the icy glare of the man just ahead of them, an immaculately dressed middle-aged man of Japanese origin. He stared at Gontran unblinkingly until he lowered his eyes, then slowly turned away, satisfied.

Turning towards the ticket window, Eugénie was so overcome by panic that she was unable to string two words together.

Marie-Amélie pushed her aside and, standing on tiptoes, bellowed: 'Four tickets for the second platform, please.'

'Why the second? The first platform is high enough,' stammered Eugénie.

'We must sign the Golden Book in the *Figaro* Pavilion, have

106

you forgotten? Papa insisted – he wants to read our names in the newspaper. Pay the lady, Aunt.'

Propelled to the back of the lift, close behind a Japanese man whose face bore an expression of childish delight, Eugénie collapsed onto a wooden bench and commended her soul to God. She could not stop thinking about an advertisement glimpsed in the *Journal des Modes* that declares: 'Do you lack iron? Are you anaemic? Chlorotic? Bravais tincture restores the blood and combats fatigue.'

'Bravais, Bravais, Bravais,' she chanted to herself.

There was a sudden jolt. Her heart in her mouth, she saw the red mesh of a birdcage passing by. She had just enough time to think, *Mon Dieu*, what am I doing here?, when the lift came to a stop on the second floor, one hundred and sixteen metres above the ground.

Claude Izner, *Murder on the Eiffel Tower*, translated by Isabel Reid

* * *

Two passages from another murder mystery, Cara Black's Murder on the Ile Saint-Louis *(one in her Aimée Leduc series), also provide some atmospheric description of the city – this time, by night.*

Aimée slid into the warm night. She saw white wavelets hitting the opposite bank of the Seine. Flooding threatened if the thaw kept up. [...]

Along the quai, a few lit windows, like eyes peering into the darkness, showed in the *hôtels particuliers*, narrow limestone-facaded town houses with delicate wrought-iron balconies and high arched entrances. Most, like hers, were attributed to le Vau, the architect of Versailles. She knew other worlds existed behind the massive carved entry doors leading to double- and triple-deep courtyards and gardens that could never be glimpsed from the outside. Life on this island took place in the courtyards, in the hidden back passages that had changed little since medieval times. The Ile Saint-Louis was a feudal island fortress, its fortifications the town houses built for the aristocracy. Five bridges spanned the comma-shaped island, which had once been a cow pasture in the Middle Ages. It was eight blocks long and three blocks across at the widest, yet so self-contained that long-time Ile Saint-Louis inhabitants – Ludociviens – still referred to the rest of Paris as "the Continent". Stubbornly reclusive, the inhabitants ignored the tourists, aware that they inhabited the most desirable streets in Paris, keeping themselves to themselves. They were proud of having allowed a post office to open only a few years ago, of having neighbors like a minister or two and like the Rothschilds, whom one was unlikely to visit to borrow a cup of sugar. Who was she to criticize. She'd never live anywhere else. [...]

Ahead, car headlights illuminated the wet pavement. She passed the Musée National d'Histoire Naturelle, a *belle époque* building Jules Verne would feel at home in – musty glass display cases of taxidermied tortoises from the Galápagos, two-headed fetuses curled in glass tubes from the year 1830. A place where she'd spent many a Saturday afternoon with her grandfather, hiding behind him to peek at the more graphic displays.

She checked her watch again and ran. A raincoated *flic* directed traffic and by the time she'd made it down the bank, littered with sand and salt to prevent slipping, to the Brigade Fluviale's headquarters, she had less than a minute to spare.

Quai Saint-Bernard, home in the summer to evening tango dancing, glimmered wet and forlorn in the lights from Pont d'Austerlitz. The slick gangplank to the Brigade Fluviale's long, low-lying *péniche* swayed over the Seine's current. She clutched the gangway rope tightly, almost losing her balance twice.

On the left loomed L'Institut du Monde Arabe. And not more than a few barges length across the Seine from it lay Place Bayre, at the tip of the Ile Saint-Louis, like the prow of a ship. White wavelets lapped against the stone steps and brushed the deserted bank.

Cara Black, *Murder on the Ile Saint-Louis*

* * *

From the sinister chill of the dark, deserted riverside to the beauty of the modest Place Furstemberg – one of the many quiet and delightful little corners of the city that are there for the finding. (And Place Furstemberg is particularly beautiful when it snows).

At number 22, rue de l'Echaudé, not far from the church of St Germain-des-Prés, there is a partly open door that, when you push it open all the way, reveals a fine eighteenth-century staircase, dark and mysterious, with a pewter jug in a niche hollowed out of the wall on the first-floor landing. I gazed for a long while at the light on those ancient stairs, incapable of moving on …

Just past there, Delacroix's studio in the tiny Furstemberg Square. The delightful sunken garden that is so good to sit in, shaded by trees on this fine summer's day, only yards from the deafening boulevard Saint-Germain. All around us, old houses with open windows, and those windows quite black. Watercolours by Delacroix, Huet, Riesener, Hugo, dreams in every direction. The oasis in our century that is so wretchedly devoid of poetry. A pale-blue sky above our heads, with clouds floating in it like puffs of steam.

Julian Green, *Paris*, translated by J. A. Underwood

* * *

And here's the 'flâneur' Edmund White telling us more about Saint-Germain – about the spirit of its famous intellectual and artistic past.

St-Germain is no longer Intelligence Central for the whole world as it once claimed to be. What made St-Germain famous internationally was the artists and philosophers just before, during and after the Second World War. In those days intellectuals and artists usually lived in hotels – dingy, crowded, under-heated little furnished rooms – and went to cafés to eat, drink, work, socialize and stay warm. As Jean-Paul Sartre, that high priest of Existentialism, recalled, he and Simone de Beauvoir 'more or less set up house in the Flore' in 1940. [...]

It wasn't all work and intellectual chat, however. As Beauvoir recalls, there were also scores of idle young people who 'were very, very bored'.

But the offices of most of the major publishing houses were nearby, the Sorbonne was a fifteen-minute walk away in one direction, and in the other there was the Chambre des Députés, the equivalent to the House of Commons. In St-Germain juries met to hand out literary prizes, movie deals were put together – and Sartre was introduced to Jean Genet for the first time on the terrace of Les Deux Magots. Le Corbusier, Giacometti, Picasso and the American Surrealist photographer Man Ray all hung out in St-Germain, partly because it was also near many of the galleries. Nightclubs such as La Rose Rouge and Le Tabou introduced bebop and *le jazz hot*.

Above all, pale young women all in black and their gaunt boyfriends in turtlenecks were presenting themselves to the passing tourists as Existentialists, which seemed mainly a matter of despairing conspicuously, carrying around a volume of *Being and Nothingness*, listening to Juliette Greco songs and drinking lots of cognacs. Albert Camus, looking as good as one possibly can in one of those fattening trench coats; Françoise Sagan, looking like a child whose puppy has just died; Alexander Calder, looking like an awakened owl – these were just some of the denizens of this celebrated neighbourhood.

Edmund White, *The Flâneur*

* * *

No trip to Paris is complete without a visit to Notre-Dame and the Louvre. Hans Christian Andersen briefly records his impressions of them in 1863 – noting, in passing, the results of the programme of urban renewal that had taken place under the direction of Baron Haussmann, appointed prefect of the Seine in 1853 and which turned Paris into the city we know today.

January 25th 1863

Went with Jonas to Notre Dame which has been completely renovated, everything around it has changed. When I was there in 1833 there were narrow old streets, now the church stands quite alone; bridges and two mighty theatres now rise by the Seine; how changed in thirty years. We went to the Louvre, saw the Egyptian rooms, mighty images of gods, marbles and mummies; went next to where clothes and everyday items of historical significance are displayed. Napoleon's hat and the hat he always wore on Saint Helena, an old worn hat. His dress as consul, the King of Rome's crib, Napoleon's camp bed, his seal; one shoe belonging to Queen Marie Antoinette, a small shoe indeed. In the evening Jonas and I went for a stroll. We came upon strange, dark and narrow streets full of old, horribly vulgar women who approached us. Then on to les Passages and home where I did some writing.

Hans Christian Andersen, *Diary*, translated by Mikka Haugaard

✳ ✳ ✳

Among the parks of Paris, the most extraordinary is the Buttes-Chaumont (from 'chauve mont' *– 'bald mountain'). Its history is considerably less attractive than the park itself: the Montfaucon gallows (immortalised in Villon's poem 'Ballad des pendus') were once sited there, and for a long time it was a lime quarry, then just an area of public waste ground. In 1862 Napoleon III decided to use it to create a park for this working-class neighbourhood, its extraordinary landscape making it the most dramatic of the*

> *city's parks. It is one of the two locations 'pondered'*
> *in detail by Louis Aragon in* Paris Peasant. *Though*
> *first published in the 1920s, the general spirit as well*
> *as the topography of the area as Aragon describes it*
> *– the journey there as well as the place itself – has*
> *changed very little.*

Certain words conjure up images that go beyond physical representation. The Buttes-Chaumont stirred a mirage in us, one with all the tangibility of these phenomena, a shared mirage over which we all felt we had the same hold. Our black mood evaporated in the light of a huge hope. At last we were going to destroy boredom […]

The taxi that was transporting us with the machinery of our dreams, having traversed the ninth and tenth arrondissements in a south-westerly north-easterly direction along the straight line of the interminable Rue La Fayette, finally reached the nineteenth at that precise point which bore the name of Germany before that of Jean Jaurès, where, at an angle of about 150° opening towards the south-east, the Canal Saint-Martin joins up with the Canal de l'Ourcq at the outlet of the Bassin de La Villette, at the foot of the great Customs buildings, at the elbow of the outer boulevards and of the overhead Métro line which reunites ridiculously those two extremes, Nation and Dauphine, in the presence of the Small Car Company, the Café de la Rotonde and the Café de la Mandoline, a few steps away from the Rue Louis-Blanc where the anarchist newspaper *Le Libertaire* has its headquarters, north of the V.D. fief and south of the undertakers' preserves, between the general stores of La Villette and the Northern Railway Company's rolling-stock repair shops, then, heading south-east, the taxi took the tree-lined Avenue Secrétan which, beyond the cinema and the General Omnibus Company, plunges through a region of schools and welfare centres constituting a triumph of secular organization. It was deserted at this hour and entirely surrendered to space, a great expanse of dead, useful masonry in which, compared with the brick and plaster walls, an air of bravado distinguished the stone of the barracks whose heights set unequal bounds to a number of local philanthropic ideas. Coming level with the Rue de Meaux we failed to notice the red dotted line which traces the border between the Quartier de La Villette and the Quartier du Combat. We had already passed the Bolivar Métro station where the Rue Bolivar is terminated by a spiral staircase, having started off among the rich pastures of new business and residential blocks. The Rue Secrétan then starts up, finally reaching the great Paving-stone depot not far from the Jacquard vocational school. Thus it is that, at the approaches to the park in which nestles the town's collective unconscious, the important factors of city life, assuming the menacing human form of postmen and middle-men, loom up out of the waste ground and out of the rag-and-bone men's and allotment gardeners' huts with all the conventional majesty and the frozen gestures of statues. At this hour, and at the speed our car was travelling, it would have been difficult to ascertain how many more opticians than usual were to be encountered in the Rue Secrétan between the Rue Bolivar and the Rue Manin, where the taxi finally came to a halt outside the chalet housing Edouard, Weddings and Banquets, which with its frieze of fretworked wood blends the style of the Black Forest to that of the Meudon industrial area.

The state of mind of the three companions, on realizing that the gates into the Buttes are open, may be left to the imagination. One of them, Noll, has never been here before, and this visit is, for him, the culmination of a day filled with superstitions, disquiet and boredom: the sudden leap of the imagination he now experiences is strengthened by the remarks being made about the garden by his two friends, who are recalling the great Suicides' bridge which, before metal grilles were erected along its sides, claimed victims even from among passers-by who had had no intention whatso-ever of killing themselves but found themselves suddenly tempted by the abyss; they are recalling, too, the Belvedere and thinking how incredible it is that they can visit the Belvedere at night, not only the

Belvedere but the lake too, and what astonishing variety is provided by this man-made arrangement of dells and running water. It is 9.25 and a thick fog has descended on the whole city. The tall lamp-posts illuminating the park with their incandescent gas jets form great sulphurous trails in this double night through which the tree trunks loom. A few boys wearing students' caps emerge from the Buttes and walk off without singing. We enter the park feeling like conquerors and quite drunk with open-mindedness.

Louis Aragon, *Paris Peasant*, translated by Simon Watson Taylor

✳ ✳ ✳

Not far from the Buttes-Chaumont park is the lively, culturally diverse district of Belleville. In the following newspaper article, My love affair with Belleville, Catherine Sanderson (known to many as the blogger Petite Anglaise) introduces us to the area she knows well as a resident.

When I began blogging as Petite Anglaise in July 2004, I'd been calling Paris home for nine years and couldn't imagine living anywhere else. I set out to write a 'Brit's eye view' of life in the City of Light and, even though my web diary gradually morphed into a far more personal story, Paris has always loomed large.

Ever since my first French lesson (at school in York, aged 11) I'd fantasised about living here, though for many years my love affair with France was little more than a long-distance crush. I made my first proper trip just before my 18th birthday, using my savings to visit a pen friend in a village near Lyons. Three years later, I worked as an assistante anglaise at a lycée in Normandy as part of my French degree.

My first trip to Paris – sightseeing with a friend – only lasted a couple of days. My most vivid memory is of our seedy hotel room near Bonne Nouvelle, which was decorated, floor-to-ceiling, in fake animal fur. Despite this inauspicious introduction, Paris worked her magic. I resolved to return, not to visit, but to stay.

Finally, my degree course behind me, I packed my belongings and took a Eurolines coach to Paris. English conversation classes would, once more, be my bread and butter, this time at the Sorbonne Nouvelle university. I found my first Parisian chez-moi – a hastily rented deux-pièces on rue de la Roquette, not far from the crowded bars of Bastille – by scouring the small ads at the American church. Although I ended up in the area quite by chance, I've been a Right Bank girl ever since, snubbing the picture-postcard quartiers in favour of the former working-class neighbourhoods of the north-eastern arrondissements. Eight years later, I moved with my French partner to Belleville, which is where I live with my four-year-old daughter today.

Hotels are rare in my neighbourhood and few tourists venture this way, even if it is a mere five stops away from Hôtel de Ville on the metro (line 11), or a five-minute bus ride (No 26) from Gare du Nord. Yet from the belvédère on rue Piat, by the entrance to the steeply downward-sloping Parc de Belleville, the widescreen panorama of the Paris skyline is every bit as stunning as the view from Sacré Coeur – and you don't have to fight your way through swathes of portrait painters and peddlers of fake watches and handbags to admire it. The only people you'll meet are nannies pushing their charges through the park or locals taking a stroll.

Belleville was once a hilltop village surrounded by farms and vineyards belonging to nearby abbeys. By the time it was absorbed into Paris proper, in 1860, it had become a large town, reputed for its guingettes, vast establishments where hundreds of revellers came to eat, drink and dance. Workers arrived in Belleville en masse when Baron Haussmann began demolishing inner-city slums in the mid–19th century, and during the workers' uprising of the Paris Commune in 1871, the last barricades to fall were in Belleville. The neighbour-hood is still home to the headquarters of the Parti Communiste Français, as well as two of France's largest trade unions.

Before I moved in, like many a visitor who leaves the metro at Belleville, I was under the impression it was Chinatown. At the busy junction by the station where four arrondissements meet (which plays host to an outdoor market on Tuesday and Friday mornings), it's true that most of the shop signs are in Mandarin and at my daughter's school there are as many Chinese children as French.

But the neighbourhood is far more culturally diverse. If you walk a few hundred metres along Boulevard de Belleville, Chinese supermarkets and snack bars soon give way to Jewish-Tunisian couscous restaurants and, in the side streets around the rue des Couronnes, corner shops sell plantains to their African clientele. Belleville has seen many waves of immigration over the past century. The most recent arrivals, in this era of spiralling property prices, are the bourgeois-bohèmes – bobos for short – a cosmopolitan crowd of affluent twenty- and thirtysomethings.

Bobos spend their time on the terrasse of Aux Folies, the Belleville bar adjacent to the former Folies-Belleville cabaret (now a discount supermarket), where Piaf and Chevalier performed. They eat out in the cosy restaurants at the top end of up-and-coming rue Rebeval, and the arty boutiques that have sprung up along boulevard de la Villette wouldn't survive without them. I know this – I'm a bobo too.

Since I began working from home, the area in which I go about my daily business has become much more circumscribed: if I drew around it on a map, the result would be a rhombus about two-and-a-half kilometres square. At the outer tips lie the Parc des Buttes Chaumont (where my daughter watches the Punch and Judy-like 'Guignol' show) and St Jean-Baptiste de Belleville church, in the shadow of which lurk my favourite fromagerie and fishmonger. Then there's Aux Folies, aforementioned, at the bottom of the hill, and the Café Chéri(e) along boulevard de la Villette.

A typical day sees me dashing to drop my daughter off at school (doors open at 8.20, closing at 8.30 with military precision) then heading to one of my favourite cafés with a newspaper. After that, if I'm feeling disciplined, I adjourn to my tiny writing studio opposite place Fréhel, where the trompe l'oeil artwork warns me, rather aptly, to beware of words (the fake billboard reads Il faut se méfier des mots). I spend my lunch break in one of the many Chinese cafés on rue de Belleville. (I won't divulge my best address; it seats approximately five.) When school's out, I'm often to be found with my daughter in one of the local parks.

What I love most is that I've been in the neighbourhood long enough now to be considered a regular. Some bar owners actually know my name. In all the 13 years I've spent in Paris, I'd never experienced such a feeling of belonging until I moved to Belleville – and I think it's safe to say I'm here to stay.

Catherine Sanderson, 'My love affair with Belleville', *The Observer*

✳ ✳ ✳

Just like Catherine Sanderson in the previous passage, for many visitors the first taste of Paris includes a room in a cheap hotel – maybe even a slightly seedy one – in essence probably not so very different from the one Julia Martin finds herself in at the start of Jean Rhys's After leaving Mr McKenzie ... *though possibly without the smell of cats.*

After she had parted from Mr McKenzie, Julia Martin went to live in a cheap hotel on the Quai des Grands Augustins. It looked a lowdown sort of place and the staircase smelt of the landlady's cats, but the rooms were cleaner than you would have expected. There were three cats – white angoras – and they seemed usually to be sleeping in the hotel bureau.

The landlady was a thin, fair woman with red eyelids. She had a low, whispering voice and a hesitating manner, so that you thought: 'She can't possibly be a French-woman.' Not that you lost yourself in conjectures as to what she was because you didn't care a damn anyway.

If you went in to inquire for a room she was not loquacious. She would tell you the prices and hand you a card:

HOTEL ST RAPHAEL
QUAI DES GRANDS AUGUSTINS
PARIS, 6ME
CHAUFFAGE CENTRAL, EAU COURANTE
CHAMBRES AU MOIS ET À LA JOURNÉE

Julia paid sixteen francs a night. Her room on the second floor was large and high-ceilinged, but it had a sombre and one-eyed aspect because the solitary window was very much to one side.

The room had individuality. Its gloom was touched with a fantasy accentuated by the pattern of the wallpaper. A large bird, sitting on the branch of a tree, faced, with open beak, a strange, wingless creature, half-bird, half-lizard, which also had its beak open and its neck stretched in a belligerent attitude. The branch on which they were perched sprouted fungus and queerly shaped leaves and fruit.

The effect of all this was, oddly enough, not sinister but cheerful and rather stimulating. Besides, Julia was tired of striped papers. She had discovered that they made her head ache worse when she awoke after she had been drinking.

The bed was large and comfortable, covered with an imitation satin quilt of faded pink. There was a wardrobe without a looking-glass, a red plush sofa and – opposite the bed and reflecting it – a very spotted mirror in a gilt frame.

The ledge under the mirror was strewn with Julia's toilet things – an ugly assortment of boxes of rouge, powder, and make-up for the eyes. At the farther end of it stood an unframed oil-painting of a half empty bottle of red wine, a knife, and a piece of Gruyère cheese, signed 'J.Grykho, 1923'. It had probably been left in payment for a debt.

Every object in the picture was slightly distorted and full of obscure meaning. Lying in bed, where she was unable to avoid looking at it, Julia would sometimes think: 'I wonder if that picture's any good. It might be; it might be very good for all I know … I bet it is very good too.'

But really she hated the picture. It shared, with the colour of the plush sofa, a certain depressing quality. The picture and the sofa were linked in her mind. The picture was the more alarming in its perversion and the sofa the more dismal. The picture stood for the idea, the spirit, and the sofa stood for the act.

Jean Rhys, *After Leaving Mr McKenzie*

* * *

Thanks to Eurostar, one of the best-known locations in Paris is probably the Gare du Nord. Step down from the train onto that platform and life seems to move up a notch. But the station has other habitués equally appreciative of its familiar grandeur. In a short novel called after the station, French author Abdelkader Djemaï gives us three retired immigrant friends who love simply to pass the time of day there.

But the place they liked best was the Gare du Nord, its pediment embellished with an inscription using Roman numerals and a round, white clock with long black hands. Above the neat design of its cornice rose twenty monumental statues, full-figured and wearing drapery. Like the three old men, time had worn them down, turned them a little grey. With crowns on their heads and heraldic shields propped against their curved legs, they represented the capitals of Europe and cities of northern France such as Arras. It was in that town's big, cobbled square pervaded by seductive arcades and suffused by the smell of chips and melted sugar, that Bonbon had once won from a fairground stall some warm blankets for the winter. In the middle of huge soft-toy animals, the wheel, studded with numbers, clubs and other playing-card symbols, had stopped on the number of the ticket he had just bought. That same afternoon, he had also tasted candy-floss.

119

As soon as they approached the Gare du Nord, they felt them-selves drawn in by its warm atmosphere, by its feminine shapes and by its soft light the colour of a good beer. It was a bit like a safe haven for them, a place to land when the mood or the fancy took them. After having crossed the cobbles of the Place Napoléon III, they had, in passing through the gates, the impression of being in the stomach of a peaceful and motherly whale. Protected by its walls with their large semi-circular windows, they remained in the station concourse, absolutely still, safe, savouring the peaceful passing of time. Who knows, perhaps they'd have a nice surprise and spot, among the thousands of travellers, a former work colleague, an old friend getting off a train or about to leave for places unknown to them and which they would no longer have the opportunity to become acquainted with.

Never having had proper homes of their own, they lingered there, in the midst of the movements of the crowd, the unending ballet of baggage, the line of advertising hoardings whose pictures regularly changed. Between the blue-and-white squares of the big window, the lamps, the newspaper kiosks and the wide stairs at the entrance to the métro, they heard the humming of machinery, the rolling of carts loaded with mail-bags, the voice of the loud-speakers, the mechanical clattering of the departure boards which, in his dream, Zalamite had found strangely blank. All this activity reassured them. They felt good beneath the immense roof supported by its elegant cast-iron pillars. Some-times a pigeon flying away out over the railway cables made them long to travel. Before, said Bartolo, trains were slower, heavier, and you heard them coming from a long way off.

Abdelkader Djemaï, *Gare du Nord*, translated by Heather Reyes

✳ ✳ ✳

From railways to canals – specifically the canal Saint-Martin, once a somewhat dark and neglected loca-tion but these days increasingly 'beautified' and often

*featured on postcards. Daniel Maximin describes it in
the form of an address to the canal itself.*

Your boundaries are two fake mountains, as artificial as you yourself: the Sacre-Coeur, raised as a warning of divine retribution and the Buttes-Chaumont, constructed through a copse of rebellious trees in a concreted deceit of naturalised channels and caves calculated to replicate nature, even to imitate its wildness.

As to your depths, they required even the metro to become airborne and greet you at Jaures then bid you farewell at the Bastille. Out of the question for the two of you to intersect underground, since the three paltry metres they dug you out did not permit you access to the mysteries of Paris. You never came to know the quaint beggars beneath your banks and bridges, and so leave the clichés of tramps and posturing lovers to the Pont-Neuf.

At the end of your route, emerging from the tunnel illuminated for the Millennium celebrations by a Japanese rainbow, Frederick Lemaitre's statue lends you one further aspect of theatricality. You'd think he were ready to stride forth across the square to the Bastille Opera, in his role as Figaro or Don Juan, ready to sing of love with or without marriage …

Finally, in the guise of an Arc de Triomphe, you were granted the July Column, memorial to the unknown rebels of the 1830 and 1848 revolutions, skirting a batch of mummies brought back from the Egyptian Campaign and never offered an obelisk of their own.

As a result, you never made your first romancers dream: *The Saint Martin Canal displayed its inky waters in a straight line, bounded by two locks. In the middle was a boat loaded with wood, and on its sides stood two rows of barrels.* It would seem that Flaubert had something better to do with his two office scriveners than to delay over detailing your décor, or to open his masterpiece by ultimately concealing his passion for writing behind the clinical coldness of mere description.

As to Balzac, forever looking for something to use, there was material enough supplied by the intriguing tale of your creation:

At the start of 1803, the construction of the St. Martin Canal was approved. Lands within the Temple district reached insane prices. The project cut the properties of the Tillet family, previously owned by Cesar Birotteau, down the middle. Then at your birth, Balzac fed his characters at your banqueting table: *you can see the long white table cloth of the St. Martin Canal, built of ruddy bricks, bordered by lime trees, and hemmed by genuinely Roman buildings in its grain warehouses .*

Romantic drownings were not relevant to your waters. From Renoir to Truffaut, tragic suicides and cinematic rescuers saved themselves for the Seine. No-one threw themselves into a canal: there you might be tipped in, murdered of an evening, fished out again the next morning, night-time corpses to settle accounts between whores and their pimps, Simenon a hundred times over, or quiet love affairs rendered permanently silent, all come to meet their end asphyxiated beneath the Lock of Death, joining a cemetery from the Merovingian era and the souls cut down from the ancient gibbet at Monfaucon.

Criminals soon abandoned their ambushes on the high roads and in the rural undergrowth, to come into the city, so that you inherited gangs of crooks, thieves and thugs, a whole other underworld, when it was decided to blame the poor for every urban malfaisance, and to limit the delinquencies of the powerful to the wealthy districts and stop them at the gates of the poor ones.

You were therefore buried at the end of your run, to make way for wide boulevards to accommodate troops deployed in suppressing popular rebellions, the peddlars of uprisings remembered today only in the ritual parades from the Place de la Republique to the Bastille, along the canalized and logical testament to former revolts: *when all humanity swarmed in stormy ferment.*

It was only thanks to a few Siberian winters that you came to attain that picture-book image of holiday leisure, with people racing across your icy surfaces, for a whole congregation of skaters without the money for skates, delighted with the Christmas gift of a free holiday.

Daniel Maximin, 'Au canal Saint-Martin',
in *Paris Portraits*, translated by Amanda Hopkinson

* * *

*And here's someone else simply enjoying the ordinary
sights of Paris on a winter's morning.*

It was almost nine o'clock when Denise reached the Pont des Arts. The crisp, clear morning set off to perfection one of the most beautiful views in Paris. She stopped halfway across the bridge, mesmerised by the sights around her. To her left lay the towers of the Palais de Justice, the spire of Saint-Chapelle and the imposing bulk of Notre-Dame with the point of the Île de la Cité and the Vert-Galant garden glinting behind them in the sunshine. To her right, far in the distance, the Eiffel Tower soared into the sky. The Seine seemed to arch its back as it curved under Pont Neuf, its current breaking against the hulls of the laundry boats before settling into a smooth yellowish flow, dotted with ducks.

She walked past the Institut and the École des Beaux-Arts, watching the second-hand booksellers and the medal traders setting up their stalls on the other side of the Quai Malaquais. She had to pluck up courage to ask a portly man the way, but he smiled at her from behind an enormous moustache and pointed out Rue de Saints-Pères.

Claude Izner, *The Père-Lachaise Mystery*

* * *

*Like any big city, Paris has long attracted people from
other cultures: they are an integral part of its richness
and variety. One of the positive results of France's past
colonial involvement with North Africa is the presence
of Arab culture in the capital and of the wonderful
Institut du Monde Arabe, on the Left Bank. A centre*

for exhibitions, conferences and concerts, as well as a library and restaurant, the views from the top are among the best in Paris. The architecture and technology of the building (including the 27,000 patterned alluminium window coverings that open and close in response to the level of sunlight) are remarkable – and the mint tea is pretty good, too. But here is Edmund White taking us on a brief visit to another Arab centre, the Paris Mosque, and then visiting the old Jewish quarter of the city.

In Paris the other pole of Arab culture is the Mosquée de Paris, across the street from the botanical garden, the Jardin des Plantes. On one side of the mosque (built in 1926), at the corner of rue Geoffroy St-Hilaire and the rue Daubenton, is what might be called the secular entrance, to the Turkish baths, the souk, the tea-room and the couscous restaurant. The *hammam* is open to men on Tuesdays and Sundays and to women the other days of the week. It is laid out in the traditional way, with a hot, steamy room, a tepid one, and a charming room-temperature chamber of cots around a tinkling fountain. The masseurs serve hot, sugared mint tea in little painted glasses as one dozes in the filtered glow of stained-glass windows. [...]

The other main entrance on the rue du Puits de l'Ermite leads into linked patios planted with roses and walkways under green-tiled arcades. The arches are finished off in carved cedarwood and supported by short red columns. Abstract, intricate tilework runs up the walls to waist height. The inner sanctum of this religious half of the mosque is the hall of worship, forbidden to non-Muslims. But every element on both sides of this complex of buildings breathes calm and spirituality, even the walled tea garden where visitors eat baklava and sip mint tea and sparrows beg for crumbs.

❉ ❉ ❉

The flâneur wanders through the Jewish ghetto in the Marais in the fourth arrondissement. Here, not far from the Hôtel de Ville in a small rectangle – bounded by the rue Vielle du Temple on the west and the rue Pavé on the east, and by the rue des Francs Bourgeois on the north and the rue du Roi de Sicile on the south – are shops selling the Torah and the Hanukkah candelabra, kosher delicatessens, the remains of an old ritual bath and two synagogues. One of them is the Synagogue Fleishman, tiny and hard to find on the rue des Écouffes, and the other is elegant and easier to spot: the Synagogue de la rue Pavée. It was built by recently arrived Polish Jews between 1910 and 1913 and conceived by Hector Guimard, the flamboyant architect who designed the stylish and distinctive *Art Nouveau* entrances to the métro.

Perhaps the best-known landmark in the neighbourhood now is Jo Goldenberg's deli and restaurant. Here, on 9 August 1982, a terrorist bomb killed six people, wounded twenty-two and blew up part of the establishment. Today these memories are virtually forgotten by visitors to the restaurant in the swirl of good food, Gypsy and klezmer music, lively talk and general animation. The walls are hung from chair level to ceiling with sketches of rabbis in prayer shawls and School of Chagall paintings of village fiddlers. It's the one place in Paris where one can strike up a conversation easily with the people at the next table.

The neighbourhood is a gathering place for eastern European Jews, with their poppy-seed cakes and strudels, as well as North African Jews, with their gooey baklavas and charred falafel. Here can be seen Hassidim in long black coats, beards and hats, standing on street corners with their hands behind their backs, discussing theology with one another. And here American Jewish tourists, fatigued with the foreignness of France, are relieved to realize that the well-posted French word *cacher* means 'kosher'. On a warm day, or on any Saturday fair or dismal, the three-block-long rue des Rosiers is so crowded with *flâneurs* that cars can barely push their way through.

Some of the visitors have come to sample the picturesque patisseries, but others are just window-shopping outside the chic new dress stores that have invaded this very old *quartier*. The neighbourhood is so popular that apartment rents are soaring.

The prosperity and sunny look of the ghetto today were not always so in evidence. Until recently this was the quarter of very poor Jews. As Cynthia Ozick has pointed out, one form that anti-semitism takes is to speak of Jews as if they are and always were rich, whereas in fact most Jews in France (and in Paris) were dreadfully poor. These poor Jews from Russia and Poland, from Alsace and later from Algeria, came to the rue des Rosiers in the nineteenth and twentieth centuries because here they could find cheap rents, a welcoming community and jobs – or news about jobs – as furriers, dressmakers, leather toolers and travelling tinkers. Here they could speak Yiddish (for very few of them spoke French at first), could worship in their synagogues, keep kosher and meet familiar faces at local cafés.

Edmund White, *The Flâneur*

* * *

And finally, a whistle-stop reminder of some of the city's highlights with Sarah Turnbull ... on the back of a motorbike. And some of the more intimate corners, too.

On previous visits to the French capital I'd rocketed up the Eiffel Tower and climbed the Arc de Triomphe and the stairs to Sacré Cœur. But with Frédéric as my guide, we mostly avoid the main monuments, spinning around them on the motorbike so that they seem merely a stunning backdrop to our adventures. Instead we revel in details. He takes me to the Marais, pointing out the dark, sculpted doorways and quaint, crooked shop fronts. He indicates the engraved plaques on façades announcing that Colette lived in the apartment above, or that on this spot in August 1944 three members of the French Resistance were shot by German soldiers. I soak up these fragments of history.

Simple discoveries seem extraordinary. Like the lovely private courtyards sealed from the street by thick wooden doors. Although at night you need the door codes to go in, during work hours you can enter by simply pressing the shiny silver buttons which are usually to the right of the entrance. One day during a stroll around the Left Bank we pass a particularly imposing ornate entry. Although it looks resolutely closed and inaccessible, when Frédéric pushes the button the door unlocks with a soft clicking sound. It's so massive we have to lean on it with all our body weight before it creaks open and we step into a leafy courtyard: an oasis of cool calm after the street noise and heat. Virginia creeper tumbles down the walls. These apartments were for nobles, Frédéric explains, pointing to the towering arched entranceway we came through which was built big enough for carriages. He indicates the mansard roof, the tall windows whose many square panes are artisanal and dimpled and so different from modern glass with its glossy sheen. Looking through them we can see high moulded ceilings. It all seems so refined. '*L'élégance française*,' Frédéric says, explaining that the essence of French elegance lies in the balance of romance and restraint.

It is August and every self-respecting Parisian has already fled to a crowded coastline. The city is full of tour groups and coaches. Seeing them only makes me more grateful for my personal guide: a Frenchman letting me in on the secrets. Who cares if his motorbike is an unglamorous old Honda? Certainly not me. Now ordinary outings are exhilarating. To Frédéric, obeying rules is only for the uncreative and we hurtle onto pavements, tackle one-way streets the wrong way, weaving wildly among traffic, alert and alive. Most thrilling of all is riding at night when millions of winking lights wake the city's monuments. The Eiffel Tower loses its metallic flatness and glows a lovely amber. Illuminated from within, the glass pyramid at the Louvre looks like a giant Scotch on ice.

I guess the circumstances are perfect for falling in love. Every skidding stop on the motorbike, each intimate garden, every candlelit café terrace conspired to spark romance. But is it the scene, the city or the man I'm succumbing to? A combination of all three? These question don't even enter my mind. Who cares when it's all so much fun. Yes, I admit, I'm carried away on a kaleidoscope of clichés straight out of a trashy romance novel. It is magic.

One evening we go for a stroll along the Pont des Arts, whose looping iron arches connect the Louvre with the gleaming gilt dome of the Institut de France. A *bateau-mouche* steams towards us on the river below, its deck crowded with waving tourists. The colours and light are Monetesque – smudged golden-pink skies and soft violet shadows. Now I see why artists and writers have compared Paris light to champagne. The evening air does have an effervescent quality. On the *quai* below, couples fall into each other's arms. I don't think I've ever seen such a meltingly romantic setting.

But Frédéric's thought are not on romance. He is beginning to wheeze, a signal that he's about to say something he finds hysterically funny. 'I would really love one day to stand here and peess on the boats,' he cackles, pretending to wave his willy at the unsuspecting families enjoying their river cruise. 'Imagine, all those poor tourists, nowhere to run or hide!' He turns to see whether I've got the joke. 'It would be so funny, no?'

Well yes, I mean I guess. Sort of. I smile vaguely. Evidently the Gallic powers of seduction are somewhat unpredictable. Unpredictable is good, of course – up to a point. But his joke takes me by surprise. Its bawdiness seems at odds with the refined appearance of the man who cracked it. Just as those comics weirdly contrasted with his shelves of highbrow books, it is hard now to reconcile the two images. Is this typically French, I wonder, this mix of culture and schoolboy coarseness? The romantic moment ricochets into the night.

Sarah Turnbull, *Almost French*

✻ ✻ ✻

Parisians – famous and not so famous

Paris has always attracted more than its fair share of the famous (as the city's cemeteries attest). Writers, artists, exiles, hopefuls of every kind – they've always flocked like moths to the City of Light. But some of the most famous Parisians never existed at all, though they can often seem more real than people we actually know. Flaubert's Frédéric Moreau, Colette's Gigi, Raymond Queneau's Zazie, and a whole host of characters created by Proust. Although they themselves are fictional, their experiences of the city come from the very real perceptions of their creators. Here's a love-sick Frédéric Moreau mooning about in 1840s Paris – remarkably like Paris today, except for the traffic and the laundry facilities ... and the absence of summer tourists.

As he had nothing to do, his idleness intensified his melancholy. He spent hours on his balcony looking down at the river flowing between the grey quays, which were blackened here and there with smudges from drains; or at a pontoon for washerwomen moored to the bank, where children sometimes amused themselves by giving a poodle a mud-bath. His eyes, leaving the stone Pont de Notre-Dame and the three suspension bridges, strayed in the direction of the Quai aux Ormes, towards a clump of old trees which looked like the lime-trees in the port of Montereau. Facing him, the Tour Saint-Jacques, the Hôtel de Ville, Saint-Gervais, Saint-Louis, and Saint-Paul rose among a maze of roofs, and the genie on the July Column shone in the east like a great golden star, while in the other direction the dome of the Tuileries stood out against the sky in a solid blue mass. It was over that way, behind the dome, that Madame Arnoux's house presumably lay.

He would go back into his room and, lying on his divan, give himself up to a vague reverie which combined working projects, plans of action, and dreams of the future. Finally, to escape from himself, he went out.

He sauntered idly up the Latin Quarter, usually bustling with life but now deserted, for the students had all gone home. The great walls of the colleges looked grimmer than ever, as if the silence had made them longer; all sorts of peaceful sounds could be heard, the fluttering of wings in bird-cages, the whirring of a lathe, a cobbler's hammer; and the old-clothes men, in the middle of the street, looked hopefully but in vain at every window. At the back of deserted cafés, women behind the bars yawned between their untouched bottles; the newspapers lay unopened on the reading-room tables; in the laundresses' workshops the washing quivered in the warm draughts. Every now and then he stopped at a bookseller's stall; an omnibus, coming down the street and grazing the pavement, made him turn round; and when he reached the Luxembourg he retraced his steps.

Sometimes, in search of amusement, he was drawn towards the boulevards. From the cool, damp air of dark alleys he emerged onto huge empty squares, full of dazzling light, where statues cast jagged black shadows on to the edge of the pavement. But soon he came upon more handcarts and shops; and the crowds made him dizzy, especially on Sundays, when, from the Bastille to the Madeleine, there was a vast torrent of humanity surging over the asphalt, in the midst of clouds of dust and a continuous din.

Gustave Flaubert, *Sentimental Education*, translated by Robert Baldick

❋ ❋ ❋

> *Two of Flaubert's more comic creations, Bouvard and Pécuchet, have an even more jaundiced view of the summertime city. Here they are, meeting for the first time at the very start of the book.*

With the temperature up in the nineties, the Boulevard Bourdon was absolutely deserted.

Further on, the Canal Saint-Martin, enclosed by the two locks, spread out the straight line of its inky water. In the middle lay a boat loaded with timber, and on the bank two rows of barrels.

Beyond the canal, between the houses separated by various builders' yards, the wide cloudless sky was broken up into bright blue pieces, and, as the sun beat down, the white façades, the slate roofs, the granite quays were dazzling in the glare. A confused murmur rose in the distance into the sultry atmosphere, and everything seemed to hang heavy with sabbath calm and the melancholy of summer days.

Two men appeared.

One came from the Bastille, the other from the Jardin des Plantes. The taller of the two, in a linen costume, walked with his hat pushed back, waistcoat undone and cravat in hand. The smaller one, whose body was enveloped in a brown frock-coat, had a peaked cap on his bent head.

When they came to the middle of the boulevard they both sat down at the same moment on the same seat.

Each took off his hat to mop his brow and put it beside him; and the smaller man noticed, written inside his neighbour's hat, *Bouvard*; while the latter easily made out the word *Pécuchet*, in the cap belonging to the individual in the frock-coat.

'Well, well,' he said, 'we both had the same idea, writing our names inside our headgear.'

'My word, yes! Someone might take mine at the office.'

'The same with me, I work in an office too.'

Then they studied each other.

Bouvard's likeable appearance charmed Pécuchet at once.

His bluish eyes, always half-closed, twinkled in his florid face. His trousers had a broad front flap and fell baggily onto beaver-fur shoes, outlining his stomach, and made his shirt billow out at the waist; and his fair hair, growing naturally in gentle curls, gave him a somewhat childish look.

His lips were pursed in a kind of continuous whistle.

Pécuchet's serious appearance struck Bouvard.

It looked as though he were wearing a wig, so flat and black were the locks adorning his lofty cranium. His whole face looked like a profile, because of the nose which came very far down. His legs, encased in narrow trousers of lasting, were out of proportion with the length of his torso; and he had a loud, booming voice.

He let out an exclamation: 'How good it would be to be in the country!'

But the suburbs, according to Bouvard, were made intolerable by the noise from the cheap open-air cafés. Pécuchet thought the same. Nevertheless he was beginning to grow tired of the capital. So was Bouvard.

And their eyes roamed over piles of building stones, the hideous water, with a bale of straw floating in it, the factory chimney rising on the horizon; sewers gave off their stench. They turned to the other side. Then they had facing them the walls of the public storehouse.

Definitely (to Pécuchet's surprise) it was hotter in the street than at home.

Bouvard urged him to take his coat off. He did not care what people might say!

Suddenly a drunkard staggered across the pavement, and speaking of workmen, they began a political discussion. Their views were the same, though Bouvard was possibly the more liberal.

Clattering over the cobbles in a cloud of dust came three hired carriages, going off towards Bercy, carrying a bride with her bouquet, solid citizens in white ties, ladies with petticoats up to their armpits, two or three little girls, a schoolboy. The sight of this wedding led Bouvard and Pécuchet to talk about women, whom they declared to be frivolous, shrewish and obstinate. Despite that, they were often better than men; at other times they were worse. In short it was better to live without them; so Pécuchet had remained a bachelor.

'I am a widower myself,' said Bouvard, 'with no children.'

'Perhaps that is your good luck.' But in the long run it was not much fun to be alone.

Then on the edge of the quay appeared a prostitute with a soldier. Pale, dark-haired and pock-marked, she was leaning on the soldier's arm, slopping along swaying her hips.

When she had moved on, Bouvard allowed himself an obscene comment. Pécuchet went very red, and, no doubt to avoid making any reply, drew his attention to a priest who was approaching.

The ecclesiastic made his way slowly down the avenue of scraggy elms planted regularly along the pavement, and Bouvard, once the tricorn hat was out of sight, expressed his relief, for he execrated the Jesuits. Pécuchet, without absolving them, showed some deference for religion.

Meanwhile darkness was falling, and the shutters opposite had been raised. More people were passing by. It struck seven.

Gustave Flaubert, *Bouvard and Pécuchet*,
translated by A. J. Krailsheimer

* * *

A twenty-first century fictional Parisian who has already achieved considerable fame (she is one of the two narrators in Muriel Barbery's award-winning novel, The Elegance of the Hedgehog*) is Renée, a concierge with a secret ...*

My name is Renée. I am fifty-four years old. For twenty-seven years I have been the concierge at number 7, rue de Grenelle, a fine *hôtel particulier* with a courtyard and private gardens, divided into eight luxury apartments, all of which are inhabited, all of which are immense. I am a widow, I am short, ugly, and plump, I have bunions on my feet and, if I am to credit certain early mornings of self-inflicted disgust, the breath of a mammoth. I did not go to university, I have always been poor, discreet, and insignificant. I live alone with my cat, a big lazy tom who has no distinguishing features other than the fact that his paws smell bad when he is annoyed. Neither he nor I make any effort to take part in the social doings of our respective species. Because I am rarely friendly – though always polite – I am not liked, but am tolerated nonetheless: I correspond so very well to what social prejudice has collectively construed to be a typical French concierge that I am one of the multiple cogs that make the great universal illusion turn, the illusion according to which life has a meaning that can easily be deciphered. And since it has been written somewhere that concierges are old, ugly and sour, so it has been branded in fiery letters on the pediment of that same imbecilic firmament that the aforementioned concierges have rather large dithering cats who sleep all day on cushions covered with crocheted cases.

Similarly it has been decreed that concierges watch television interminably while their rather large cats doze, and that the entrance to the building must smell of pot-au-feu, cabbage soup or a country-style cassoulet. I have the extraordinary good fortune to be the concierge of a very high-class sort of building. It was so humiliating for me to have to cook such loathsome dishes that when Monsieur de Broglie – the State Councillor on the first floor – intervened (an intervention he described to his wife as being 'courteous but firm', whose only intention was to rid our communal habitat of such plebeian effluvia), it came as an immense relief, one I concealed as best I could beneath an expression of reluctant compliance.

That was twenty-seven years ago. Since then, I have gone every day to the butcher's to buy a slice of ham or some calves' liver, which I slip into my net bag between my packet of noodles and my bunch of carrots. I then obligingly flaunt these pauper's victuals – now much improved by the noteworthy fact that they do not smell – because I am a pauper in a house full of rich people and this display nourishes both the consensual cliché and my cat Leo, who has become rather large by virtue of these meals that should have been mine, and who stuffs himself liberally and noisily with macaroni and butter, and pork from the delicatessen, while I am free – without any olfactory disturbances or anyone suspecting a thing – to indulge my own culinary proclivities.

Far more irksome was the issue of the television. In my late husband's day, I did go along with it, for the constancy of his viewing spared me the chore of watching. From the hallway of the building you could hear the sound of the thing, and that sufficed to perpetuate the charade of social hierarchy, but once Lucien had passed away I had to think hard to find a way to keep up appearances. Alive, he freed me from this iniquitous obligation; dead, he has deprived me of his lack of culture, the indispensable bulwark against other people's suspicions.

I found a solution thanks to a non-buzzer.

A chime linked to an infrared mechanism now alerts me to the comings and goings in the hallway, which has eliminated the need for anyone to buzz to notify me of their presence if I happen to be out of earshot. For on such occasions I am actually in the back room, where I spend most of my hours of leisure and where, sheltered from the noise and smells that my condition imposes, I can live as I please, without being deprived of the information vital to any sentry: who is coming in, who is going out, with whom and at what time.

Thus, the residents going down the hall would hear the muffled sounds that indicated a television was on, and as they tend to lack rather than abound in imagination, they would form a mental image of the concierge sprawled in front of her television set. As for me, cosily installed in my lair, I heard nothing but I knew that someone was going by. So I would go to the adjacent room and peek through the spy-hole located opposite the stairs

135

and, well hidden behind the white net curtains, I could inquire discreetly as to the identity of the passer-by.

With the advent of videocassettes and, subsequently, the DVD divinity, things changed radically, much to the enrichment of my happy hours. As it is not terribly common to come across a concierge waxing ecstatic over *Death in Venice* or to hear strains of Mahler wafting from her lodge, I delved into my hard-earned conjugal savings and bought a second television set that I could operate in my hideaway. Thus, the television in the front room, guardian of my clandestine activities, could bleat away and I was no longer forced to listen to inane nonsense fit for the brain of a clam – I was in the back room, perfectly euphoric, my eyes filling with tears, in the miraculous presence of Art.

Muriel Barbery, *The Elegance of the Hedgehog*,
translated by Alison Anderson

✳ ✳ ✳

Among the new voices being heard in Paris are those of young people from the high-rise suburbs, where first and second generation immigrants make up the greater part of the population. The area's potential for talent and energy has made itself felt in recent years through award-winning films and some extraordinary new writing. Here is publishing phenomenon's nineteen-year-old Faïza Guène giving us the distinctive voice of her narrator, Doria, recounting a visit to the Eiffel Tower.

Seeing as Mum's still on holiday till next week, we decided to wander round Paris together. It was the first time she'd seen the Eiffel Tower for real, even though she's been living half an hour from it for almost twenty years. Before now, it was just something on the TV news on New Year's Eve, when it's all lit up and underneath it people are partying, dancing, kissing and getting wasted. Whatever, she was bare impressed.

'It must be two or three times our block, isn't it?'

Straight up, I told her. Except our block and the estates round here generally don't get so much tourist interest. It's not like you find camera-toting Japanese mafia standing at the bottom of the tower blocks in this neighbourhood. The only interested ones are journalists and they just spin big fat lies with their sick reports about violence in the suburbs.

Mum would of happily spent hours looking at it. Personally, I think it's ugly, but you can't deny it's there. The Eiffel Tower is like this big statement. I'd like to of gone up it in the red and yellow lifts, ketchup-mayo style, but it was too expensive. And another thing, we'd of had to queue up behind the Germans, the Italians, the English and loads of other tourists who aren't scared of heights or spending their cash. We didn't have enough money to buy a miniature Eiffel Tower either. They're even uglier than the original but still, it's classy to have one on your telly. Tourist-trap stalls are so expensive. Plus what those guys sell is total crap. After that, this pigeon shat on my shoulder. I tried wiping myself against a statue of Gustave Eiffel 1832–1923, but the bird shit had gone hard and wouldn't shift. In the RER train, people were staring at the mark and I felt *hchouma*. I was this fed up because it's the only jacket I have that doesn't make me look poor. If I wear any of the others, everybody calls me 'Cosette' from *Les Misérables*. Anyway, who cares, whether it shows or not I'll still be poor. Later, when my boobs are bigger and I'm a bit cleverer, when I'm a grown-up you get me, I'll join an outfit that helps people …

It does my head in knowing there are people who need you and you can be useful to them.

One of these days, if I don't need my blood or one of my kidneys, I could donate them to sick people who've had their name on the list for the longest time. But I wouldn't just do it for a clear conscience, so I could look myself in the eye when I was taking off my make-up after work, but because I really wanted to.

Faïza Guène, *Just like tomorrow*, translated by Sarah Adams

❊ ❊ ❊

An earlier generation of immigrant voices can be heard in Abdelkader Djemaï's tender and graceful Gare du Nord. Here we accompany the three old friends, Bonbon, Bartolo and Zalamite, on their daily stroll around Paris.

Bonbon, Bartolo and Zalamite had only seen the Eiffel Tower and the Champs-Élysées once or twice, and had never glided down the Seine in a *bateau-mouche*. They made their way along the streets as if condemned always to follow the same itinerary, the same stops, to see the same trees in the square again, to pass again and again in front of buildings they'd walked past for years and years. Only the telephone boxes seemed to change their appearance. Behind their thick glass they welcomed different occupants, calm or agitated, impassive or smiling. They saw them from the back, in profile, face on, squatting, the receiver glued to their mouth, a satchel or bag at their feet.

Each day they passed people from every country and of every colour, tourists in shorts or under umbrellas, climbing with their cameras up towards Sacré-Coeur and the Place du Tertre. There were also bustling shoppers, pick-pockets, drug dealers, prostitutes of both sexes, people strolling with their dogs, those just watching the world go by, workers stuffing sandwiches.

The three old men never ate in the street. They thought it just wasn't done, that it wasn't acceptable behaviour. And they didn't understand either why dogs and cats were so pampered. More spoilt than the children of the rich, fed like kings, they were in evidence everywhere, all along the pavements and round the foot of the plane-trees. They had beauty salons, wardrobes, very pretty collars, clinics and cemeteries just for themselves. The luckiest went on holiday abroad. Vaccinated and all dolled up, they travelled by plane or boat in a nice cosy cage. [...]

Bonbon, Bartolo and Zalamite began their itinerary on the central reservation above which ran the aeriel section of the metro, line number two between Nation and Porte Dauphine. They always obeyed the traffic-lights. After the pedestrian crossing on the Boulevard Barbès, one of the most used in the whole capital, they slowly went up the Boulevard Rochechouart, then came back down it again. When they felt up to it, they pressed on as far as the Place Clichy. They walked alongside little restaurants open to the traffic fumes, past tourist coaches, newspaper kiosks, merry-go-rounds, shooting galleries, scruffy shops, and sex-shops with eye-catching windows. Now and again, Bartolo stopped to tighten his belt, Bonbon to wipe his nose and Zalamite to get his breath back or tie his shoe-laces.

Their clothes tidy, their cheeks always shaved, and walking at the same pace, they also went along the Boulevard de la Chapelle, passed close to the hammam tucked away at the far end of a porch, took the rue Marx Dormoy before turning left into rue Jean-François Lépine. Past the nursery school, which was older than they were, they crossed the metal bridged striped with graffiti, went into the square and, with aching legs, got back to the stone benches where they rested for a long time. They didn't want to look like the many people with nothing to do or those who simply didn't have enough money to sit down at a café table. They avoided standing about, their backsides glued for hours to the metal railings running along by Tati's and the Louxor, the cinema, now closed, where, at one time, they used to go. Between its walls hung with red fabric Bonbon had discovered a taste for choc-ices.

Near the bus stop, the square sometimes took on the look of a village square. When it was fine, it rang with bursts of laughter, shouts of children. In the shade of the acacias, the grown-ups exchanged their memories and worries and what remained of their hopes. Beneath the jerky gaze of pigeons, others slowly rolled a cigarette or read their newspapers, shaking their heads.

Even if they did not buy anything, the three friends loved to pass their Sunday mornings at the Porte de Clignancourt market. They took their time hovering among the stalls and the vans with sliding sides. They felt rolls of fabric, tested the thickness of a jacket's lapel, the depth of a pocket, the sturdiness of a seam or a frying-pan. They sniffed the spices, felt the neck of a pear, the belly of an aubergine and tapped the backs of different kinds of melons. They were amused by the gullibility of people mesmerised by the three-card trick, surprised by the exorbitant prices charged for old furniture by antique dealers, and discovered the existence of exotic fruits or objects they'd never seen before.

Abdelkader Djemaï, *Gare du Nord*, translated by Heather Reyes

❊ ❊ ❊

Among the many eminent foreigners to have taken up more or less permanent residence in Paris, the avant-garde writer and art collector Gertrude Stein (1874–1946) was surely one of the most famous. A friend to the geniuses of Modernism, she and her companion were at the shaping heart of the capital's artistic life for the first half of the twentieth century. Here she is, in her inimitable style, pretending to be her devoted companion, Alice B. Toklas, writing her autobiography and describing the delights of a visit to their friend Picasso.

Gertrude Stein and I about ten days later went to Montmartre, I for the first time. I have never ceased to love it. We go there every now and then and I always have the same tender expectant feeling that I had then. It is a place where you were always standing and sometimes waiting, not for anything to happen, but just standing. The inhabitants of Montmartre did not sit much, they mostly stood which was just as well as the chairs, the dining room chairs of France, did not tempt one to sit. So I went to Montmartre and I began my apprenticeship in standing. We first went to see Picasso and then we went to see Fernande. Picasso now never likes to go to Montmartre, he does not like to think about it much less talk about it. Even to Gertrude Stein he is hesitant about talking of it, there were things that at the time cut deeply into his spanish pride and the end of his Montmartre life was bitterness and disillusion, and there is nothing more bitter than spanish disillusion.

But at this time he was in and of Montmartre and lived in the rue Ravignan.

We went to the Odéon and there got into an omnibus, that is we mounted on top of an omnibus, the nice old horse-pulled omnibuses that went pretty quickly and steadily across Paris and up the hill to the Place Blanche. There we got out and climbed a steep street lined with shops with things to eat, the rue Lepic, and then turning we went around a corner and climbed even more steeply in fact almost straight up and came to the rue Ravignan, now Place Emile-Gondeau but otherwise unchanged, with its steps leading up to the little flat square with its few but tender little trees, a man carpentering in the corner of it, the last time I was there not very long ago there was still a man carpentering in the corner of it, and a little café just before you went up the steps where they all used to eat, it is still there, and to the left the low wooden building of studios that is still there.

We went up the couple of steps and through the open door passing on our left the studio where later Juan Gris was to live out his martyrdom but where then lived a certain Vaillant, a nondescript painter who was to lend his studio as a ladies dressing room at the famous banquet for Rousseau, and then we passed a steep flight of steps leading down where Max Jacob had a studio a little later, and we passed another steep little stairway which led to the studio where not long before a young fellow had committed suicide, Picasso painted one of the most wonderful of his early pictures of the friends gathered round the coffin, we passed all this to a larger door where Gertrude Stein knocked and Picasso opened the door and we went in.

Gertrude Stein, *The Autobiography of Alice B. Toklas*

✳ ✳ ✳

Some of the most famous Parisians are those who adopted the city – through choice or exile or, quite often, a chosen exile. Oscar Wilde ended his days there: broken by persecution and imprisonment for homosexuality in England, he sought the liberal ethos and beauty of Paris, staying in the humble Hôtel d'Alsace. In The Last Testament of Oscar Wilde, *novelist and historian Peter Ackroyd movingly recreates Wilde's final months through an imagined diary. (Wilde's tomb – sculpted by Jacob Epstein – is one of the most visited in the Père-Lachaise cemetery. It has become famous for the lipstick kisses lovingly bestowed upon it by Wilde devotees.)*

9 *August 1900*

Hôtel d'Alsace

This morning I visited once again the little church of St Julian-le-Pauvre. The curé there is a charming man who believes me to labour under a great sorrow; once, he approached me on silent feet and whispered as I knelt before the altar, 'Your prayers may be answered by God's grace, monsieur.' I told him – I could not whisper – that my prayers have always been answered: that is why I come to his church each day in mourning. After that, he left me in peace. […]

As I left the little church this morning, three young Englishmen passed me. I have grown accustomed to such encounters, and adopted my usual posture. I walk very slowly and take care not to look in their direction: since I am for them the painted image of sin, I always allow them the luxury of protracted observation. When they had retreated to a safe distance, one of them turned around and called back at me, 'Look! There goes Mrs Wilde! Isn't she swell?' I walked on with flaming cheeks and, as soon as they had turned the corner of the rue Danton, I hastened back to my room here, my nerves quite ruined. I still tremble as I write this. I am like Cassander of the pantomime, who receives blows from the harlequin's wand and kicks from the clown. […]

So it is that the English treat me as a criminal, while my friends continue to regard me as a martyr. I do not mind: in that combination I have become the perfect representative of the artist. I have all the proper references. I am Solomon and Job, both the most fortunate and the least fortunate of men. I have known the emptiness of pleasure and the reality of sorrow. I have come to the complete life – brilliant success and horrible failure, and I have attained the liberty of those who have ceased to develop. I look like Mrs Warren but without, alas, the profession. [...]

I picked up the *Mercure* the other day, and it was there in the middle of the paragraph of unbearable French. I put down the newspaper as if it were in flame. I could not look at it. It was as if in that name, Oscar Wilde, there was a void in which I might fall and lose myself. A madman sometimes stands on the corner of the rue Jacob – opposite the café where I sit. He cries out at the cabs as they pass by and splatter him with mud. No one could know so well as I the agony and bitterness that force him to speak in bewildered words. But I have learned the simple lesson: I am one of the damned who make no noise.

[...] Maurice is a wonderful friend. I met him by absurd chance. I happened to be in the bookshop behind the opera-house when I saw him scrutinizing the shelf devoted to modern English literature. I knew from long experience that a volume of my *Intentions* lay there, and waited impatiently to see if he would take it down. Alas, he opened something of an explicit nature by George Moore.

I could restrain myself no longer, and I approached him. 'Why,' I asked, 'are you interested in that particular author?'

Maurice was quite unabashed. 'I live by the café where he says he learned French, the Nouvelle Athènes.'

'Well, it is a disgrace that such a place is allowed to remain open. I shall speak to the authorities about it tomorrow.'

He laughed and I knew at once that we were going to be great friends. He told me that his mother was French and his father English, but that his father was dead. It is true, I said, that English people tend to die with unerring regularity. He was astonished by my candour. Of course he did not know who I was: his father had not mentioned my name to him, not even on his death-bed. But I can forgive anything of those who laugh, and I decided to educate Maurice myself. I introduced him to my friends and, occasionally, I allow him to buy me dinner.

On these summer afternoons we lie on my narrow bed and smoke cigarettes. He has heard from the wind and the flowers that I was once a great writer, an artist of international reputation, but I do not think he believes them. Sometimes in an unguarded moment I will describe a fiery-coloured scene from *Salomé* or repeat a more than usually apposite epigram. Then he gives a curious side-long glance as if I were speaking of someone whom he does not know.

'Why do you not write now?' he asks me.

'I have nothing whatever to say, Maurice, and in any event I have said it.'

Peter Ackroyd, *The Last Testament of Oscar Wilde*

✳ ✳ ✳

Among the many colourful writers associated with Paris is the poet Paul Verlaine. In his 1895 Confessions of a Poet, *he recounts the tragi-comic consequences of a little too much* vie bohème.

For three days after the interment of my beloved cousin I lived on beer, and on beer alone. When I got back to Paris, as if I weren't already miserable enough, my superior gave me a dressing down for the extra day's leave I'd taken and I told him to mind his own damned business. I'd turned into a drunkard and, as the beer in Paris was so awful, I'd taken to absinthe – absinthe in the evening, absinthe at night. Mornings and afternoons were given over to the office, where I was liked no better on account of my outburst. And what's more, out of deference to my mother and my superior, I had to keep both of them in the dark about my new and despicable habit.

Absinthe! How awful to remember those past days, as well as the more recent ones which are still too recent for my dignity and my health – and, when I reflect upon it, especially for my dignity.

Just one draught of that vile sorceress (what idiot promoted it into fairy or muse?) – one draught was amusing, but then my drinking led to more spectacular outcomes.

I was in possession of a key to a flat in Batignolles where my mother and I continued to live after the death of my father, and I used it to return home at whatever time of night I chose to. I'd tell my mother lies as long as my arm, and she never suspected – or maybe she *did* suspect but forced herself to turn a blind eye. Alas! Her eyes are closed for good, now. Where did I pass the nights? Not always in very respectable places. Often, passing 'beauties' chained me up with 'garlands of flowers', or I passed hour upon hour in THAT HOUSE OF ILL REPUTE so masterfully described by Mendes; I shall mention it again at the proper time and place. I used to go there with friends, among then the much lamented Charles Cros, and be swallowed by the taverns of the night where absinthe flowed like the rivers Styx and Cocytus.

Early one beautiful morning (though for me it was a woeful one) I returned, surreptitiously, to my room, which was separated from my mother's by a passageway, undressed quietly, and got into bed. I needed an hour or two's sleep, not earned, but from the point of view of human kindness, deserved. I was still sound asleep at nine o'clock when I should have been getting ready to go to the office and drinking my broth or hot chocolate. My mother came in, as usual, to wake me up.

She let out a loud exclamation, as if wanting to laugh, and said (for the noise had roused me), 'For God's sake, Paul, what *have* you been doing? You obviously got drunk again last night.'

The word 'again' hurt me. 'What do you mean "again"?' I said, bitterly. 'I never get drunk, and yesterday I was even less drunk than usual. I had dinner with an old friend and his family; all I drank was a weak red wine and, after dessert, coffee *sans* cognac, and I got in rather late because it was a long way from here. I slept peacefully, as you can see.'

My mother didn't say a word, but from the latch of the double window she unhooked my little shaving mirror and held it in front of my face.

I had gone to bed wearing my top hat.

Paul Verlaine, *Confessions of a Poet*, [1895] translated by Erica King

✳ ✳ ✳

In this delightful piece by Gérard de Cortanze, a young boy is introduced to some famous Parisians of the past through the vivid memories of an old lady recalling her heady youth in Montparnasse.

... suddenly my godmother enquired, 'Do you know Montparnasse?'

'No, Godmother', I replied, surprised at the incongruity of the question. Then, anxious to embellish my statement, I added, 'I have not had the honour of making the acquaintance of Tonparnasse – I mean, your Parnassus ... '

When the howls of laughter unleashed by my answer died down my godmother, noting that my education was still lacking in certain respects, turned to my parents and, in tones which brooked no possible contradiction, proposed, 'How about we take our coffee at the Coupole? The weather is fine so let us make the most of it. And my godson will get to see my Parnassus ... '

A few minutes later I was savouring what would subsequently become one of my most beautiful memories. We entered the vast interior of the café-restaurant-dance hall, with its classical lines and the pillars covered with paintings I found extravagant but which utterly absorbed my attention. My godmother explained that the decoration of these thirty-two pillars had been assigned to thirty-two painters who, in return for their labours, received unlimited credit in the purchase of drinks, and who then spent the rest of their lives downing glasses of *absinthe* at the bar. She seemed able to recognise the author of each work: here was something executed by Chantal Queneville; there, by August Clerge; a little further on, a Pierre Dubreuil; at the end on the left, Othon Friesz; just behind you, Marie Vassillieff ... 'In the 1920s, artists coming down the hill from Montparnasse – known as the *Montparnos* – were made welcome here at the crossroads of the Boulevards Raspail and Montparnasse ... ' Transported on waves of enthusiasm, my godmother was inexhaustible. I had never seen her like that before and never would again – so alive, so joyous, so happy. We stayed there until nightfall, and there passed before my eyes Modigliani, Derain, Matisse, Kisling, Zadkine, Chagall, Foujita, Man Ray, Clavé, César, Zao Wou-Ki, and many many more ... . She who never took anyone into her confidence, actually disclosed that she had attended a masked ball at Montparnasse in 1925. Someone had taken a photo of Foujita in a grey bowler hat, flanked by the artists Feder and Leopold Levy, and seated on Marcel Grün's knees: 'Ah, her ... he so loathed that slovenly Bohemian that he sought to compensate by dressing with excessive fastidiousness: always in top hat and buttercup yellow gloves. You need to know that the whole world knew him as poverty-stricken, and people would throw him *sous* and sugar lumps ... ' She promised to show me the photo the next time I came to visit her. Yet I was never to see her again, so she could never again talk to me of Montparnasse, where she had crossed paths with Soutine, who 'in spite of all his success, his well-cut suits and his manicured nails, retained the air of a kicked cur.'

Gérard de Cortanze, 'Le Géorama de Montparnasse',
from *Paris Portraits*, translated by Amanda Hopkinson

* * *

Among the many famous non-French Parisians, two of the most influential were certainly American Sylvia Beach and Irishman James Joyce – and each has ensured the continued fame of the other. It was Beach, founder of the original 'Shakespeare and Company' bookshop, who undertook to publish Joyce's Ulysses. *A radical in relationships as well as literature, it was with the help and encouragement of her partner Adrienne Monnier that Beach opened the bookstore whose descendant has featured on other pages of this anthology.*

To sustain her celebrated bookshop, Shakespeare and Company, Sylvia Beach depended on the Anglo-American trade so abundant in the tourist twenties but in steep decline as the thirties turned somber. It was as if the Parisians had recaptured their city from the American visitors: the Montparnasse cafés were no longer populated by a predominant French clientele and fewer Americans found their way up from the place de l'Odéon on boulevard St. Germain to the literary landmark at 12 rue de l'Odéon, the street – "as restful as a little street in a provincial town" – Shakespeare and Company had "Americanized". So popular had the bookshop become that Americans departing for France gave 12 rue de l'Odéon as their forwarding address and writers known to Sylvia Beach were given credit and loans in French francs (until their dollars came through) at what Sylvia began to call her Left "Bank", or the Odéon Bourse. Although the Depression was slower to reach France, Shakespeare and Company was feeling the effects of the Wall Street crash well in advance of other Parisian enterprises, and Sylvia Beach might be said to seek credit and loans herself.

Sylvia had long enjoyed a certain commercial overflow and decided cultural overlap from a French bookshop at number 7 on the same narrow thoroughfare. This was Adrienne Monnier's La Maison des Amis des Livres; the proprietor and Sylvia were devoted to one another. Their long-standing affair of the heart dated from the first encounter, when plump Adrienne in a skirt down to her ankles (her traditional costume "a cross between a nun's and a peasant's") chased Sylvia's Spanish hat down the rue de l'Odéon, blown off by the wind.

"*J'aime beaucoup l'Amérique*," declared Adrienne, to which Sylvia replied, "*J'aime beaucoup la France*." Thus the Franco-American liaison was forged, an attachment as substantial and enduring as that of Gertrude Stein and Alice Toklas.

Adrienne had first seduced Sylvia to the book business, and encouraged and helped her establish Shakespeare and Company, first on nearby rue Dupuytren, and then opposite her own shop on bookish rue de l'Odéon, a duplicate book-shop across the street.

Now that the American trade had diminished so drastically, Shakespeare and Company depended on attracting a French following, but a Frenchman (like Erik Satie, who called Sylvia Beach "Mees") was there to absorb the literary atmosphere, to browse or borrow from the lending library but not buy. One prominently displayed item did draw French and American alike – this was James Joyce's monumental novel *Ulysses*, in 1930 still banned in England and America but openly available at Shakespeare and Company. *Ulysses* was now in its eleventh edition, proudly published by Sylvia Beach.

Throughout the 1920s James Joyce had surrendered his literary affairs (as well as many domestic and personal responsibilities) into the willing hands of his publisher. Little could Sylvia have known the consequences of her spontaneous offer, after having known Joyce only a few days: "Would you let Shakespeare and Company have the honor of bringing out your *Ulysses*?" Having suffered persecution and prosecution for many years over his completed masterpiece, Joyce accepted this opportunity "imme-diately and joyfully". The novel was a work of genius, Sylvia knew, but she could not have known the sacrifice genius demands in its service, or the all-consuming requirements of those enlisted in the "Joyce industry". Most likely Sylvia would have proposed to publish *Ulysses* even if she had known (except for the sad deceptive ending to her relationship with Joyce) what she was in for. Perseverance, loyalty, devotion were fixtures of her nature. Joyce was equally persevering, but he reserved loyalty and devotion for his immediate family.

As the 1930s got under way, Joyce entered his most demanding phase, the self-interest covered by a show of impeccable courtesy (after ten years, Sylvia was still "Miss Beach", or, in a playful mood, "Madame Shakespeare", while Joyce remained forever "Mr. Joyce") when issuing a barrage of demands in the form of requests, usually for funds "by 'tomorrow,' 'by express,' 'by return of post.'" Sylvia's working hours at Shakespeare and Company were from nine A.M. until midnight, the larger part of her responsibility concerned with the care and feeding of her *enfant terrible*, Mr. Joyce.

William Wiser, *The Twilight Years: Paris in the 1930s*

❊ ❊ ❊

A leap forward of more than half a century and we're in mid–90s Paris where, in Cara Black's Murder on the Île Saint-Louis, *a group of Parisians are engaged in one of their favourite activities: demonstrating. And, of course, the usual reception committee awaits them ...*

Darkness shaded the narrow cobblestone surface of the Left Bank street. Fewer than a hundred had gathered for the march; Krzysztof had expected more. And the press? Not a single camera crew in sight.

Disappointed, he wiped damp hair from his forehead, passing a candle to the next demonstrator. The march would culminate two blocks away in a peace vigil on the grounds of l'Institut du Monde Arabe, the cultural foundation where the conference was being held. A multistorey building part library, museum, and seminar centre, l'Institut du Monde Arabe's countless bronze light-sensitive shutters imitated the *moucharabiya*, an Arab latticework balcony. Another Pompidou design project not working half the time.

He looked for Orla, who'd promised to provide them with more information, but she was late as usual. A camera truck from France2 pulled up. He brightened; now they'd get coverage on the television news. The word would spread.

Fellow Sorbonne students wearing bandannas strummed guitars, and the old Socialists, always ready for a demonstration, circulated bottles of red wine among those standing in loose ranks. Handheld candles illuminated expectant faces. He smiled at his fellow organizer, Gaelle, who had draped a red-and-white Palestinian scarf over her tank top. She raised her fist in a power salute, grinning back as he dumped an empty candle box in a bin.

'My press contact's coming. I told him you'd convinced Brigitte and MondeFocus to sponsor this demonstration,' Gaelle said, her face flushed with excitement.

Perfect, everything was running according to plan. His nervousness evaporated. Now he was sure everything would work. He'd followed the right channels, applied for and obtained a permit. There was not even a *flic* or a police car in sight.

A girl with long blonde hair smiled and kissed him on the cheek, her scent of patchouli oil surrounding them both. 'Comrade, help out a minute, won't you?'

He caught a whiff of kerosene and hoped no one had brought a lantern. Their march was supposed to end in a silent protest illuminated only by hundreds of flickering candles as they submitted their alternative proposal. A lantern would ruin the effect.

She smiled up at him and slung her backpack strap over his shoulder. 'Take this, will you? I've got to carry the rest of the candles.' The clink of bottles came from within the backpack. She winked. 'I've brought something to quench our thirst while we keep vigil.'

He hesitated and shrugged. 'Why not?' He hefted the bag.

Voices around him rose in song and he recognized 'The Internationale', the old Socialist anthem. He found himself stepping out in time with the singing. And then she vanished, dropping behind the ranks of marchers, as someone hugged him.

The group linked arms and strode over the cobbles. Beside him, Gaelle held the green STOP THE OIL DRILLING banner aloft.

As they marched, their voices and laughter echoed off the stone buildings. Their candles flickered in the soft breeze from the Seine. His uncle's speech came to his mind. Proud of his ancestry? *This* made his heart swell with pride.

They reached the corner and rounded it. Ranks of uniformed CRS, Compagnies Républicaines de Sécurité, an armed riot squad, stood in front of l'Institut du Monde Arabe.

Cara Black, Murder on the Île Saint-Louis

✻ ✻ ✻

And staying with Cara Black, a short visit to the typical student accommodation where her protagonist lives. (Anyone who's been a student in Paris will recognize it …)

Krzysztof Linski was the name she'd found listed in the phone directory at an address on the rue d'Ulm. He lived in a sand-coloured stone building near the Panthéon, a few doors down from the Institut Curie and the Lebanese Maronite Church. The ground floor contained a bar/pub with posters advertising heavy metal and rockadelic nights. Bordering the nearby Sorbonne, this was a student area, the Latin Quarter. The building had no elevator but there was a flight of wide red-carpeted stairs with oiled wood banisters, leading to apartments containing lawyers' and psychiatrists' offices. The staircase narrowed to bare wooden steps as it reached the sixth floor, which held a row of *chambres de bonnes*, former maids' rooms.

Typical cramped student accommodations. Hovels was more descriptive, she thought. A shared hall toilet; the odour of mildew coming from the dirt-ingrained corners. Peeling floral wallpaper illuminated by a grime-encrusted skylight that let in only a sliver of light. Dust motes drifted in it and she sneezed. The chords of an amplified electric guitar reverberated from down the hall.

Cara Black, *Murder on the Île Saint-Louis*

✷ ✷ ✷

Now a famous fictional Parisian. One of the many unforgettable characters created by Proust is Albertine. In her novel of that name, Jacqueline Rose lets Albertine tell her story from her own point of view. Here she is indulging in a little retail therapy in one of Paris's most famous department stores – though it turns out to be somewhat less relaxing than envisaged …

I have always preferred the department stores to the expensive boutiques which line the arcades. There the shop assistants seem too close to the outside, tropical fish opening and shutting their mouths in what I always read as disbelief, as if they can see exactly how much money I have in my purse, staring out at me as hard as I stare in. On my way back from his apartment, I liked, as I often had before I knew him, to loiter in front of la Samaritaine. I could pretend that nothing had changed. Because it touches the river, it marks the turning point where I know I have left his world behind. I cross over the Pont Neuf and go down the rue Dauphine before catching a tram to the thirteenth district, past the Gare d'Austerlitz and into the narrower streets which run behind the Place d'Italie, where I live.

Only a few steps away from the river, la Samaritaine sits facing the Seine, which offers its grand façade a vast, perfectly reflecting sheet of glass. At certain times of the day the light hitting the windows makes their display of goods and gowns almost invisible. All the onlookers on the pavements can see is themselves, with the river moving slowly behind. Gazing into the black panes and watching my reflection bounce off the water, I feel as if I am plunging into the sea.

On this particular day I had decided to make a detour, cutting over the Pont de la Concorde before heading up the Boulevard Raspail to le Bon Marché, which had long been one of my haunts. Not as classy as other newer stores like le Printemps, perhaps, but what I love about it is the crush. In le Bon Marché everyone mingles – the bored, chintz-covered wife of the banker, metal boots clinking on the flagstones, spending his small change and more; the baron self-consciously flicking back his tailcoat as he retreats into the library for the afternoon; the boa-feathered mistress of the famous writer, who, as part of the deal between them, has lodged her in an apartment with a direct view on to ladies' fashions from the other side of the street. When you first walk in, a vast structure of glass and steel dazzles the eyes. A thousand chandeliers hang from every level, vast rectangular mirrors suspended from the landings double the space and brightness in all directions, as though you were at a theatre where the stage lights, turned on full, have been suddenly flooded into the audience. Then slowly you notice that everyone is moving, brushing and touching each other untroubled by any distinctions of wealth and class. Apparently in a terrible hurry, they hold on fast to their bags and purchases as if they might otherwise drop them or, putting them down for a second, walk off and leave them behind. Now I am standing in a grand station. Hemmed in by the crowd but with no-one in attendance, I dream I am going backwards on one of my childhood journeys and tearing out of France.

You can spend all day at le Bon Marché, but I was happy with an hour or two at the tail end of the afternoon. As soon as I step onto the black and white paving, I feel a sense of grandeur. One of a million, elbowing the crowd and jostling, but not for attention, I pick up twill and damask and brocade, chintz and lace and lamé silk. Fabrics exciting because they are formless so that anyone is free to imagine them transformed into fantastical shapes. I always buy something. If only a piece of chenille or a run of frosted gold thread. Or once, for a cream satin dress I had tired of, a silk cashmere wrapper of American indigo.

It was a few weeks into our liaison. On this particular day I had wandered up and down an aisle on the ground floor stocked with ribbons, purses, and haircombs, little bits and pieces which I loved to drop over myself, pushing pieces of gem-studded tortoiseshell into my hair, showering myself with deep pinks and violets and greens. I was holding a white cambric fan with, on one side, a deep yellow lily and the other, a purple rose. Twirling it between my fingers, back and forth, in front of a mirror to see how it suited me. Slowly I became aware of another presence, with a stillness which stood out from the busying, indifferent, crowd. Reflected in the mirror before me and multiplying my image to infinity, one of the long rectangular mirrors suspended over the central gallery just caught the corner of my elbow and the backward sweep of my skirt. And then a dark shape, someone who – from the position of the shadow thrown from the far side of the gallery – had to be situated out of my immediate sight, but very close to me. I spun round in time to see a tall man in a grey serge suit and soft felt hat, which almost blended into the samples of curtains draped behind him to the floor. He moved sideways, instantly wiping his figure from the glass.

I put back the fan as one caught stealing. And then travelled through every aisle of every floor of the building, all round the central gallery, partly in panic, but partly to find him or at least, by stopping and loitering as one does of course at le Bon Marché, to test – from a rhythm that would exactly halt and keep pace with mine – if he was coming after me. I stepped out into the fading six o'clock evening light of the city and felt his steps echoing behind me on the pavement.

Jacqueline Rose, *Albertine*

* * *

Hans Christian Andersen loved to meet other writers.
During his 1833 visit to Paris he stayed at 71 rue de
Richelieu, where Stendhal had once lived. In The Fairy
Tale of My Life, *Andersen remembers his encounters*
with Alexandre Dumas, dramatist and novelist best
known for The Count of Monte Cristo *and* The Three
Musketeers.

The jovial Alexandre Dumas I usually found in bed, even when
it was long past midday; here he would lie with pen, paper
and ink writing his latest play. One day I found him thus. He
nodded in a friendly way and said, 'Sit down, wait a minute;
I'm just being visited by my muse. She'll be leaving soon!' He
wrote and talked loudly. Next he shouted, 'Viva!', jumped out
of bed and said, 'The third act is finished.'

He lived in the Hotel des Princes in rue de Richelieu; his wife
was in Florence, his son, the young Dumas who later became a
writer too, had his own apartment in town.

'I live just like a *garçon*,' Dumas would say. 'You have to
accept me as I am.'

One evening he took me to several different theatres so I
could experience life back-stage. We went to the Palais Royal,
spoke to Dejazet and Anais, wandered arm in arm down the
colourful boulevard to the Theatre St. Martin.

'Now they will be just in their underclothes – time to go up!'
said Dumas. This we did, backstage and behind the curtains, and
into a sea worthy of a thousand and one nights. A throng of people
was there: men doing the props, those involved in the chorus,
dancers too. Dumas led me straight into the heaving crowd.

Hans Christian Andersen, *The Fairy Tale of My Life*,
translated by Mikka Haugaard

✢ ✢ ✢

And finally, here's Julian Green trying to pin down
the feelings of ordinary Parisians for the city that is

their home. The details may have changed over the
years, but even in the twenty-first century the spirit of
his observations remain valid.

Paris is a city that might well be spoken of in the plural, as the
Greeks used to speak of Athens, for there are many Parises, and
the tourists' Paris is only superficially related to the Paris of
the Parisians. The foreigner driving through the city from one
museum to another is quite oblivious to the presence of a world
he brushes past without seeing. Until you have wasted time in a
city, you cannot pretend to know it well. The soul of a big city is
not to be grasped so easily; in order to make contact with it, you
have to have been bored, you have to have suffered a bit in those
places that contain it. Anyone can get hold of a guide and tick off
all the monuments, but within the very confines of Paris there is
another city as difficult of access as Timbuktu once was.

I call it a secret city because foreigners never enter it, and
I am tempted to call it sacred, because its sufferings make it
dearer to us. Parisians know it so well and find its existence so
natural that they never even dream of talking about it – except
for novelists and poets, of course, whose job it is to see as if for
the first time, through completely fresh eyes, things to which
we pay no attention. Even they do not always succeed in telling
us clearly what they have discovered. They may, for instance,
describe everything about a little café near the rue de Buci, but
it takes the special sensitivity of a Baudelaire or a Proust to give
us what is nowadays called its atmosphere, to convey the charm
of a certain kind of ugliness, and to render the indefinable sense
of companionship that flows from the objects characterising
a place only the inattentive find ordinary: the plant adorned
with a dreadful red ribbon, the worn leather bench spewing
out tufts of black horsehair, the solid white marble tabletop,
the oilcloth writing pad and the penholder that have served to
write so many declarations of love and fine words of parting,
and beside them the pale blue siphon – the ritual accessories of

café life as portrayed in a painting by Picasso or Derain. And, in a way, that is Paris. Everything in this city has a quality that defies analysis but enables you to say without hesitation: 'That is Paris' – even if it is only a milk can dangling from a door knob, or one of those coarse brooms sweeping up the leaves at the pavement's edge in October with a sound like the sea, or an array of tired-looking volumes in a bookseller's box on the embankment between the pont Neuf and the pont Royal. Why this should be so I do not know, but Paris sets its seal on everything that belongs to it. The tourists are too distracted or in too much of a hurry to notice it, but the heart of the true Parisian will beat faster, if he is away from Paris, at the memory of a few pots of flowers on a windowsill, or a popular refrain whistled by a butcher's boy as he cycles by. Show him a photograph of a baker's shop with a child eating a croissant, or a photograph of a table or a chair on a pavement with a waiter standing beside them in his white apron, a towel under his arm, and he will think: 'That is neither Toulouse nor Lyon nor Marseille, though the casual observer might be deceived. That is Paris. Good or bad, what Paris produces is Paris, be it a letter, a bit of bread, a pair of socks, or a poem. What we give the world, we have borrowed from no one; it is ours. It may be taken from us, stolen from us, but imitated? – never.'

Julian Green, *Paris*, translated by J. A. Underwood

❊ ❊ ❊

Cities of the dead

Because Paris has attracted – and helped to foster – so many famous people, its main cemeteries – Père-Lachaise, Montparnasse and Montmartre – have become tourist attractions in their own right. It's also possible to visit the Catacombs to which the bones of the ancient cemetery of Saints-Innocents were removed when the numerous dead began to threaten the health and very life of the living. In Paris: The Secret History, *Andrew Hussey 'tells it like it was'.*

The stench of central Paris was notorious. The reason for this was that by the early nineteenth century the cemeteries of Paris, many of which dated back to pre-Roman times, were dangerously over-crowded. The most ill reputed of these was that of the Saints-Innocents in the heart of the city. This place had long been famous, at least by night, as the haunt of necromancers, whores, drinkers, thieves and, throughout the eighteenth century, grave-robbers who sold the freshest corpses to students and professors in the École de Médicine across the river. The cemetery of Saints-Innocents […]

was also a place to be avoided whenever possible. It had reached a gory apogee during the Revolutionary Terror when baskets of severed heads and headless bodies were regularly and unceremoniously dumped at its edges. Its very smell – rich, deadly and overpowering – was the foulest reminder of the recent, murderous past.

In 1776, the common grave, into which the poor of Paris had been flung like so much garbage over the centuries, began to subside; dead bodies began to appear in rotten lumps, breaking through the cellar walls of nearby houses alongside flesh-eating rats. Many of these houses were on the point of collapse and their inhabitants were suffocating in the foul, sulphurous air. In 1780, several people died in the rue de la Lingerie of a mysterious pestilential infection caused by 'bad air'.

It was not until the early 1800s that the decision was taken to destroy Saints-Innocents, along with all the other smaller local cemeteries of Paris, and to open three large spaces for the dead, of which the largest was Père-Lachaise, on the outskirts of the city. The bones of Saints-Innocents were to be removed to Denfert-Rochereau, the old quarry that had provided the stones for the new city. The early years of the nineteenth century, the so-called 'century of light', were marked by the night-time manoeuvres of corpse-carriers, shifting the bones of the dead from one end of the city to another, trailed by a retinue of priests intoning prayers for the dead. A journalist who protested that this was a desecration of the city's deceased ended up in prison, indicating that there was also a specifically political aspect to the activities.

More to the point, the old quarries and underground tunnels that were revealed at the end of the eighteenth century were rumoured to be harbouring revolutionaries and insurrectionists, a literal underground force that might rise up at any time and seize the city. Better to block the gaps with the useless dead.

Andrew Hussey, *Paris: The Secret History*

* * *

A cemetery – especially one as vast and laden with history as Père-Lachaise – is the perfect setting for crime and mystery stories. Here's a little scene-setting from near the start of Claude Izner's The Père-Lachaise Mystery. Though set at the end of the nineteenth century, modern-day visitors will easily recognise it from the description given through the eyes of a young maid-servant left to roam the cemetery alone for an hour and a half while her mistress keeps a rendezvous with a mysterious man.

The carriage entered the cemetery gates moments ahead of a funeral cortège and proceeded down one of the looped avenues. The rain formed a halo of light above the vast graveyard. On either side of the avenue was a succession of chapels, cenotaphs and mausoleums adorned with plump cherubs and weeping nymphs. Among the tombs was a maze of footpaths and avenues invaded by undergrowth, still relatively sparse in these early days of March. Sycamores, beeches, cedars and lime trees darkened an already overcast sky. […]

'You will remain here. He wishes to see me alone. I shall return in an hour and a half.'

'Oh, Madame, please. It'll be dark soon.'

'Nonsense, it's not yet four o'clock. The gates close at six. If you don't want to rise ignorant, you've plenty of time to visit the tombs. I recommend Musset's, over there in the hollow where they've planted a willow. I don't suppose you know who he is. Perhaps you'd better go up to the chapel. It'll do you no harm to say a prayer.'

'Please, Madame!' implored the young girl. But Odette de Valois was already walking away briskly. Denise shivered and took shelter under a chestnut tree. The rain had turned to drizzle and a few birds had resumed their singing. A ginger cat moved stealthily amongst the tombstones […]

She was suddenly reminded where she was when she came upon a dilapidated, pseudo-Gothic mausoleum adorned with interlocking names. She walked over to it and read that the remains of Héloïse and Abélard had lain there since the beginning of the century. Was it not strange that her memories of Ronan had brought her to the tomb of these legendary lovers?[...]

Denise was wandering, lost, in the Jewish part of the cemetery. She walked past the tombs of the tragedienne Rachel, and Baron James de Rothschild [...]

Finally she got her bearings. There in front of her stood the memorial cenotaph to André Chenier, built by his brother Marie-Joseph. She read one of the epitaphs, finding it beautiful: *'Death cannot destroy that which is immortal.'*

Musing over the words in an attempt to forget how dark it was becoming, she turned right. She had no watch, but her inner clock told her it was time to go to the meeting place. When she arrived, there was no one there. She stood for a while, shivering with fright and cold. Her shawl was soaked through by the fine rain. Finally, she could wait no longer. She ran back up the avenue. She remembered from a previous brief visit with her mistress that the chapel dedicated to the de Valois family was a little further up, a few yards from the tomb of the astronomer Jean-Baptiste Delambre. She cried out as she ran:

'Come back, Madame, I beg you! Saint Corentin, Saint Gildas, Holy Mother of God, protect me!'

At last she could see the funerary chapel where a faint light was glowing. Looking anxiously around, she began to walk cautiously towards it. All of a sudden, a shadow darted out of a bush, chased by another. Two cats.

'Madame ... Madame. Are you there?'

Claude Izner, *The Père-Lachaise Mystery*,
translated by Lorenza Garcia and Isabel Reid

✳ ✳ ✳

One of the most famous residents of the Père-Lach-aise cemetery is Doors' singer Jim Morrison. At one

*time the authorities even had to provide a permanent
guard for it. Travel writer and broadcaster Jennifer
Cox makes a date with the singer, who died in Paris
in 1971, still in his twenties.*

I've always been fascinated that Jim Morrison – a parallel Elvis:
sexy, iconoclast gone to seed – ended his days in Paris. Erotic
and playful as he, Paris was also cultured and subtle. As the
Lizard King became the Lard King and tired of himself, maybe
that was what drew him there.

I suspect that as a boyfriend Jim Morrison would have been
an absolute nightmare: unfaithful, self-indulgent and often
cruel. But he was also a lithe sex god who created the sound-
track to my teen years, and the affinity I felt with him ran deep.
I decided to spend the day with him at his grave in the stately
Père Lachaise cemetery, to try and pinpoint the attraction.

Père Lachaise was the most visited cemetery in the world and
has been a fashionable address for the afterlife since its incep-
tion in 1804. It was Napoleon who converted what was originally a slum neighbourhood into a vast cemetery, arranging to
have Molière reburied here at the 'launch party'. Its reputation
as the 'in' place for the 'over' crowd thus established, its million
residents now included Gertrude Stein, Edith Piaf, Oscar Wilde,
Pissarro and Proust. But as you made your way up from the
metro, the proliferation of signs, maps and memorabilia over-
whelmingly pointed to Jim Morrison being the grave célèb here.

Finding Jim Morrison's grave was quite tricky: Père Lachaise
still had all the winding avenues and tree-lined boulevards from
the days when people lived (rather than died) here and it was easy
to get lost. Getting lost wasn't such a hardship though, as the
cemetery was a moving and beautiful site: tombs varied from Art
Deco Egyptian pharaohs and larger-than-life muscular bronze
angels to austere black granite obelisks, painstakingly scrubbed
mirror-clean by stooped middle-aged women every single day.

Like Cemetery Number 1 in New Orleans, this was a place

where the living had an ongoing relationship with their dead. And nowhere was this more true than at Jim Morrison's grave. [...]

Turning the corner of a wide boulevard, hidden amongst the headstones and next to a large tree trunk, I found Jim. Or rather the crowd around Jim.

Three nineteen-year-old boys were camped on one of the tombs, the ubiquitous backpackers' banquet of plain French bread and Orangina spread before them, plus an assortment of boxed CDs and Walkmans. Two were baseball-capped, fresh-faced Americans, the other a baggy-jumpered, straggly-haired Frenchman. They had one set of headphones between them and were taking turns, passing it round like a joint.

'"LA Woman" ... that's my favourite song. Maaan this song is amazing,' said the first young American, transported by the music in his headset. [...]

But their discussion was suddenly disrupted by a furious Frenchman bursting from between the trees and marching over: '*Ce que faites-vous ici?*' he bellowed. 'What is wrong with you that you are sitting on the burial place of the dead eating your lunch? Have you no respect?' [...]

In the five hours I stayed by or near the grave, around a hundred people visited. The Frenchman was right to say that the tourists were insensitive but he was wrong to say they lacked respect. It was the very reason they were there: out of love and respect.

Jim Morrison's grave was unimposing. A plain, squat head-stone stated without fuss that James Douglas Morrison lived from 1943 to 1971. The grave itself was a shallow granite frame around a sandy pit, maybe 3ft by 6 ft.

Every mourner stepped up to the grave with a sense of the theatrical, individual players each featuring in their own one-act drama. A group of Latino boys in gang insignia, silently regarding the grave, their heads bowed in fresh grief as if Jim Morrison had died yesterday, not 30 years ago. The tallest of the group took a bottle of bourbon from his bag. Passing it between them, they each took a swallow. Taking an extra swallow, the leader then poured a measure directly onto the grave before placing the bottle gently on the headstone. Standing straight, he touched two fingers to his heart, his lips, then onto the headstone. One by one each of the gang repeated the sequence. Ritual completed, without a word they turned and walked away.

A Midwestern couple in their forties pointed to the grave and poignantly told their three teenage children: 'When we were your age, he meant everything to us. We wanted you to meet him.'

A woman in her twenties, dreadlocked and comprehensively tattooed, stood in the shadows, looking angry and smoking a joint. With each deep inhalation she stared moodily at Jim's grave, her face a furious mask of intimate thoughts. Watching disdainfully as the latest group left, with an angry sigh she stalked over to the deserted grave. Standing before it thoughtfully, she took one last drag on the joint then flicked it burning into the grave. It landed on a single red rose and immediately melted through the plastic wrapping, coming to rest amongst the fragile petals. It glowed for a moment, one amongst the litter of cigarettes and half-smoked joints that already made the grave resemble a pub ashtray at closing time. She watched until it dimmed and died, then, muttering something inaudible, slunk off into the maze of graves.

Finding a lull in the mourners, I put down my bag and walked over to the grave myself. It wasn't just bourbon bottles and cigarettes, the grave was full of poems and dedications, some written on purple metro tickets: [...]

As I read the dedications, I wondered why I – and all these other people – nurtured such enduring love for Jim Morrison? The Love professor had described successful, healthy relationships as ones in which our positive traits are reflected back by our chosen partner. By choosing Jim Morrison, were we claiming some part of his creative, sexual vitality as our own? By liking Jim were we saying we were like Jim?

Or could it simply be that we didn't want to forget how good it felt to be young, passionate, misunderstood and alive? Music is a powerful memory and mood trigger and Jim Morrison was a Door that took us back to that time and state.

Jennifer Cox, *Around the World in 80 Dates*

❋ ❋ ❋

As well as being a depository for the remains of the famous, and consequently a place of pilgrimage, Père-Lachaise is also the resting place of ordinary Parisians. With a brief nod at the beauty of the place, Jean Follain (1903–1971) describes the other side of the cemetery's reality – including the crematorium.

Père-Lachaise, scene of the Communards' last stand, remains imbued with the odours of the nineteenth century when several out-lying villages became part of Paris. Monsieur Thiers, the dwarf with the powerful brain – the print of whose apotheosis still adorns some old rural dwellings – is buried there beneath an immense square mausoleum. A few of the graves of Napoleon's generals are still tended; many no longer are. The lover of emotions, his jacket collar covered in dandruff, discovers old, muddied wreaths, and traces, with broad-tipped finger, the eagles carved in relief upon the mossy stone.

The vast array of monuments, amphorae and crosses twists the heart on sunny days of abundant vegetation while, in the corners not yet cleared of weeds, poppies and wild oats sway: there's a patch like this not far from the Communards' Wall.

Around the crematorium, the columbarium forms a huge library of urns. Godless *petits bourgeois* (who, in life, wore an expression both stubborn and sweet-natured) and workers – sober men of conviction – have themselves cremated. In order to pay their respects to the ashes, their relatives must, if they are placed high in the wall, take a ladder and climb up to the numbered compartment, one among so many others.

One can visit the crematorium. The cremation room bears the stamp of solomonic architecture. It includes an organ. The coffin is placed in a stuccoed mock-oven decorated with roses, then removed, behind the scenes, and slid, in the presence of only two relatives, into the real oven which consumes almost everything because among the ashes one can find only a few fragments of bone.

During public visits, the crematorium furnace does not operate at full power; I witnessed, among the visitors, a *petite-bourgeoise* woman dressed in black, the pink glow lighting up her face, laughing as she cried out, 'Well, I, who love the heat, I'll be all right!'

But widows who believe in the resurrection of the body have had constructed, in Père-Lachaise, some hideous tombs to their late husbands; one of them consists of an enormous tower rising into the sky in the form of a factory chimney; another is adorned with huge symbolic women, their eyes closed.

Sometimes a couple of old businessmen, sitting on a bench next to one of the pathways, discuss, in loud voices, the water-tightness of the terrain, in anticipation of their future tombs. They envisage the possible depredations caused, around their corpses, by the infiltration of underground water, while the birds, in a last ray of sunlight, look for Francis of Assisi.

Jean Follain, *Paris*, translated by Annie Woodward

✻ ✻ ✻

Still a focus for high political feeling, the Communards' Wall is a much-visited corner of Père-Lachaise. The working-class uprising known as the Paris Commune came hot on the heels of the Franco-Prussian war when starvation and hardship were suffered particularly by the city's poor. It is the custom for those with leftist leanings to place red roses at the Mur des Fédérées *– and occasionally one can see there a vast wreath, moved from the tomb of a rich bourgeois or high-ranking government official to be propped against the wall where so many ardent rebels died. Historian Andrew Hussey gives a vivid snapshot* *of the event which has made the place so famous. The annual pilgrimage to the wall takes place on 28th May.*

The Commune's last stand was in the cemetery of Père Lachaise, at the centre of the working-class district of Belleville. The last defiant but doomed defenders were cut down in the passageways between the tombs of the writers Balzac, Nerval, Nodier and Delavigne. The surviving Communards were lined up against the eastern wall of the cemetery and shot. This spot became a favoured place of execution for 'suspects', who were rounded up over the next few days and months and sliced up by the new technology of the machine-gun, which could kill hundreds a day without unduly fatiguing the executioners. Across the city, behind high walls and in public, the bodies of Communards were heaped without ceremony. Sightseers who could stand the stench tripped over nearly a thousand bodies laid out in the Trocadéro. It had been raining for days and the streets were now muddy, dangerous labyrinths, still obscured by smoke and home to the last fugitive Communard snipers or patrolling Versaillais death squads. The atmosphere among the supporters of Versailles was loud and smug with triumph: Charles Louandre, a journalist and 'enemy of the people', declared that it was a blessing to see an end to 'this orgy of power, wine, women and blood known as the Commune'.

The last barricade was broken in the rue Ramponneau in Belleville on 28 May. One lone sniper held off the Versaillais troops for several hours before disappearing, unknown and still free.

Andrew Hussey, *Paris: The Secret History*

❋ ❋ ❋

In the presence of the dead, even the most sophisticated find themselves re-assessing their lives and relationships. Glamorous American actress Madison, in Kate Muir's Left Bank, *becomes introspective beside the shared grave of philosopher-novelists Jean-Paul Sartre and Simone de Beauvoir in Montparnasse cemetery.*

Now they are beside the shared grave of de Beauvoir and Sartre by the far wall. Olivier, though not a religious man, does like to worship his god whenever possible, and stands by Sartre's tombstone in wordless communication. De Beauvoir's fans are by far the most enthusiastic, Madison notices as she takes off her hat. They have left flowers, notes, and more mysteriously, old *Métro* tickets and single rolled cigarettes: essentials in the after-life. She feels a sudden desire to pick one up and sit on Simone's grave to smoke it, but she hasn't touched a cigarette since Sabine returned. To keep her mind off the craving, she teases Olivier.

'Perhaps, after twenty years, you should think of dropping the black-suit, white-shirt thing except for funerals. What about some autumnal tones? They would suit your complexion.' She points to a postcard propped up on Sartre's grave. 'Even *he* wore dirty-old-man raincoats, and at the height of fashion, those dreadful mock-suede car coats with fur collars.'

'You know that my exterior is of no importance to me,' says Olivier grandly, who recently threw a hissy fit when Luiza slightly singed the collar of his designer white silk shirt while ironing. 'I only require simplicity, like a monk.'

'Yeah, right,' says Madison, laughing. But she is also looking at the two names together for ever on the simple headstone – Sartre above, de Beauvoir below some years later – and wondering if she would want to share a public eternity with Olivier. She knows too well that Sartre and de Beauvoir had their contingent loves, but they were soulmates. She can't say that about Olivier. Not any more. Nor does she want contingent loves for herself. No Paul Rimbauds, no desire to be anyone's mistress. No desire for deception.

Kate Muir, Left Bank

✻ ✻ ✻

The creator of Gigi, Colette, was buried in Père-Lachaise in 1954, after a State funeral – the first woman to be accorded such an honour. But it was

> *Montmartre cemetery – the third and slightly less visited,*
> *by tourists, of the 'big three' in Paris – that she chose*
> *to describe in this short piece written over forty years*
> *earlier. It is dated just after the festival of All Saints, the*
> *traditional day for families to visit their forebears.*

6 November 1913

This place holds no secrets, yet it is not without its surprises.
The throngs of people, the flowers, the children being dragged
along – it has a busy, Sunday-ish feel to it, not very reverent.
All these people seem to have come along, as I have myself, in a
spirit of indifference. I don't 'know' anyone here. The Caulain-
court bridge, which shakes when the trucks and buses cross
over it, does nothing for the funereal grandeur of the place. This
is just an odd sort of garden, a toy-town consisting of midget
houses, chapels like huts, and mausoleums like shacks, all built
out of massive stone, iron, or marble, all fashioned and carved
in cheerful bad taste and with a childish self-importance which,
instead of winning you over, makes you shrug and give a cynical
laugh, turning the ritual visit into an indecent sort of outing.

How to describe the enamelled, chocolate-coloured fortresses
decorated with mouldings and small round windows, except
that they are like the entrance to Magic City? And whatever are
we to make of those yellow ceramic rings stuck on the railing or
leaning against the blocks of granite? There are some on almost
every tomb. The Living throw them to the Dead like rings of
toasted golden bread, never again to be crunched by those tooth-
less, lipless mouths. 'Here, have another one! Catch this! You
can have another next year!' We can't give them all real flowers,
there wouldn't be enough to go round. In this one cemetery
alone there are so many, so many Dead. They encroach on the
paths, jostle for space, suddenly halt the living in their tracks by
squashing them in between two railed enclosures which almost
touch one another. But this is of no concern to the Living, be
they man or woman, who squeeze through with some irritation,

pulling back their coats, just as they might in a crowded department store ... .

So many Dead. Yes, under this bridge, next to the road, beside us, among us. Here the Dead are so close, and not much covered by the wood, the lead, the earth. Wood crumbles away, lead goes into holes, the earth sucks in air ... I do not quite shiver, but I am chary of this lush soil sticking to my shoes. I am suspicious of the smell in the wind, I loathe the idea of the charnel house being allowed to exist here in the midst of the city, lying in between a new hotel and a picture palace ... When our time comes and we ourselves, obedient, joyous, and ready, have to make that leap, to destroy and purify and scatter our own disgusting remains, let our charnel house be Fire.

But then what would become of the cult of the Dead, as understood by that good lady over there standing in a proprietorial manner over her small patch and treading all over one, two, three, four slabs engraved with names and dates? She is giving the neck of an urn a thorough going-over with her little brush, scratching the moss away, sweeping it up, pinching out a late shoot from the rose bush, muttering under her breath and clicking her tongue. 'Tut, tut, these servants!' Then she picks up her brush and her gloves again, checks her hat is on straight, examines her reflection in the convex medallion of a string of pearls, and off she goes, with a look of disgust at the luxuriant ivy, thorns, and russet brambles freely establishing their stranglehold on an abandoned green tombstone.

> Colette, 'Montmartre Cemetery', in *Paris Tales*,
> translated by Helen Constantine

❊ ❊ ❊

Kate Mosse's monumental and absorbing novel Sepulchre *begins in Montmartre Cemetery, its atmosphere on a bleak March day perfect for launching readers into the mystery that unfolds from the funeral described.*

WEDNESDAY 25TH MARCH 1891

This story begins in a city of bones. In the alleyways of the dead. In the silent boulevards, promenades and impasses of the Cimetière de Montmartre in Paris, a place inhabited by tombs and stone angels and the loitering ghosts of those forgotten before they are even cold in their graves.

This story begins with the watchers at the gates, with the poor and the desperate of Paris who have come to profit from another's loss. The gawping beggars and sharp-eyed *chiffonniers*, the wreath-makers and peddlers of *ex-voto* trinkets, the girls twisting paper flowers, the carriages waiting with black hoods and smeared glass.

The story begins with the pantomime of a burial. A small paid notice in *Le Figaro* advertised the place and the date and the hour, although few have come. It is a sparse crowd, dark veils and morning coats, polished boots and extravagant umbrellas to shelter from the unseasonable March rain.

Léonie stands beside the open grave with her brother and their mother, her striking face obscured behind black lace. From the priest's lips fall platitudes, words of absolution that leave all hearts cold and all emotions untouched. Ugly in his unstarched white necktie and vulgar buckled shoes and greasy complexion, he knows nothing of the lies and threads of deceit that have led to this patch of ground in the 18th *arrondissement*, on the northern outskirts of Paris.

Léonie's eyes are dry. Like the priest, she is ignorant of the events being played out this wet afternoon. She believes she has come to attend a funeral, the marking of a life cut short. She has come to pay her last respects to her brother's lover, a woman she never met in life. To support her brother in his grief.

Léonie's eyes are fixed upon the coffin being lowered into the damp earth where the worms and the spiders dwell. If she were to turn, quickly now, catching Anatole unawares, she would see the expression upon her beloved brother's face and puzzle at it. It is not loss that swims in his eyes, but rather relief.

172

And because she does not turn, she does not notice the man in grey top hat and frock coat, sheltering from the rain under the cypress trees in the furthest corner of the cemetery. He cuts a sharp figure, the sort of man to make *une belle parisienne* touch her hair and raise her eyes a little beneath her veils. His broad and strong hands, tailored in calfskin gloves, rest perfectly upon the silver head of his mahogany walking stick. They are such hands as might circle a waist, might draw a lover to him, might caress a pale cheek.

He is watching, an expression of great intensity on his face. His pupils are black pinpricks in bright, blue eyes.

The heavy thud of earth on the coffin lid. The priest's dying words echo in the sombre air.

'*In nomine Patri, et Filii, et Spiritus Sancti.* Amen. In the name of the Father, the Son, and the Holy Ghost.'

He makes the sign of the cross then walks away.

Amen. So be it.

Léonie lets fall her flower, picked freshly in the Parc Monceau this morning, a rose for remembrance. The bloom spirals down, down, through the chill air, a flash of white slowly slipping from her black-gloved fingers.

Let the dead rest. Let the dead sleep.

The rain is falling more heavily. Beyond the high wrought-iron gates of the cemetery, the roofs, spires and domes of Paris are shrouded in silver mist. It muffles the sounds of the rattling carriages in the Boulevard de Clichy and the distant shrieks of the trains pulling out from the Gare Saint-Lazare.

The mourning party turns to depart the graveside. Léonie touches her brother's arm. He pats her hand, lowers his head. As they walk out of the cemetery, more than anything Léonie hopes that this may be an end to it. That, after the last dismal months of persecution and tragedy, they might put it all behind them.

That they might step out from the shadows and begin to live again.

Kate Mosse, *Sepulchre*

* * *

Past tense

Is it possible to write the history of a city? – especially when that city is Paris. Colin Jones' introduction to his PARIS: Biography of a City is actually headed, 'Writing the Impossible History of Paris'. Here's what he has to say.

In 1975 the avant-garde writer Georges Perec undertook to record what took place in a single Parisian square in a period of less than twenty-four hours, spread over three consecutive October days. In his *Tentative d'épuisement d'un lieu parisien* (1975), – 'Notes Towards an Exhaustive Account of a Parisian Site' – Perec explained that he chose the Place Saint-Sulpice in the Sixth arrondissement for his experiment. The site was moderately well equipped with the adornments of a modern city: a town-hall, a tax office, a police station, three cafés (one of which was also a tobacconist), a cinema, a famous and historic church, a publisher, a funeral parlour, a travel agent, a bus stop, a tailor, a hotel, a fountain, a newspaper kiosk, a shop selling religious objects, a parking lot, a beautician – 'and lots of other things'. His aim, however, was to leave all these out of his range of vision and to describe the rest – 'what happens when nothing happens except the passing of time, people, cars and clouds.'

The chronicle runs to nearly sixty pages. It is written in a terse, lapidary, informational style.

> Three children being taken to school. Another apple-green *deux-chevaux* car.
> The pigeons fly round the square again.
> A 96 bus passes, stops at the bus-stop (Saint-Sulpice section);
> Geneviève Serreau gets off the bus and takes the Rue de Canettes. I call out to her, knocking on the café window, and she comes to say hello.
> A 70 bus passes.
> The church bell stops.
> A young girl eats half a cake.
> A man with a pipe and a black bag.
> A 70 bus passes.
> A 63 bus passes.
> It is 2.05 p.m.

The experiment 'concludes':

> Four children. A dog. A little ray of sunshine. The 96 bus. It is 2 o'clock.

Perec's efforts to chronicle a Parisian site 'exhaustively' – covering the equivalent of less than a day in the life of the empty spaces of a single Parisian square – yielded a small book.

Let us now examine, through Perec's prism, the task confronting historians who undertake to write the history of the whole city of Paris, rather than a fleeting moment in the life of a single urban square within it. History is normally defined as a discipline which records what happened in the past (and not only the passage of 'time, people, cards and clouds'). And in the history of Paris a lot has happened. Thus in writing its history we historians try to achieve rather more than Perec's aim chronicling, in a single location, 'what happens when nothing happens'. Yet we find ourselves facing the following daunting 'facts' about our subject (which I set out in Perequian manner):

175

number of squares: 670
number of streets and boulevards: 5,975
length of public highways: 5,959 kilometres
number of municipal buildings: 318
number of fountains: 536
number of public monuments: 40,000
number of shops: 62,546
number of buses: 4,364
number of bus routes: 275
number of bus-stops (*banlieue* excluded): 1,754
number of taxis: 14,900
number of traffic lights: 10,800
number of cafés: 2,050
number of hairdressers: 2,845
number of beauty parlours: 67
number of funeral parlours: 157
number of pigeons: 60,000
number of dogs: 200,000
number of public conveniences: 498
kilometrage of visitable underground tunnels: 300
number of individuals resident in the city of Paris: 2.1
million
number of private households: 1.1 million
length of history: more than 2,000 years (excluding
the prehistoric era)
possible number of individuals who have ever lived in
Paris or just passed through, each
with their own histories: ... countless

It is tempting to conclude from such somewhat hallucinatory statistics – of squares, streets, houses, buses, pigeons, dogs, people and so on – that writing the history of Paris is an impossible quest [...] one can never write an exhaustive history of a city as ancient, diverse and complex as Paris.

Colin Jones, *Paris: Biography of a City*

* * *

Like any big city, some things in Paris change over the years, some stay the same. The Soleil d'Or brasserie (once the haunt of avant-garde artists and poets such as Apollinaire), which crops up in Claude Izner's The Père-Lachaise Mystery, *still exists at 1 Place Saint-Michel – though today it goes by the less vivid name of Café du Départ.*

The amber light of the street lamps of Boulevard Saint-Michel illuminated a bustling crowd of penniless students, teachers and bohemians of all types, drifting towards the café terraces where absinthe, that goddess of dreams and oblivion, could be imbibed. From there they ogled the ankles of the young women holding up their skirts to keep them from sweeping the trampled snow as they made their way to dinner, or hurried towards the omnibus stand near the ornamental fountain.

The Soleil d'Or, Number 1 on Place Saint-Michel, on the corner of the quay, was an ordinary brasserie that attracted a stream of bearded, long-haired and unfashionably dressed young men. Some had disreputable women, faces caked with powder, on their arms.

Victor followed them. A staircase behind the counter led down to the basement decorated by Gauguin. Furnished with a piano, trestle tables and chairs, which were now piled with hats, the cellar smelt of cigars, pipes and cheap scent. On arrival, the artists rested their canvases against the walls and then ordered an aperitif from the sulky waiter leaning on the bar.

Claude Izner, *The Père-Lachaise Mystery*
translated by Lorenza Garcia and Isabel Reid

✳ ✳ ✳

Another place which still exists, though with certain 'modifications', is the famous Folies-Bergère. Here is J.-K. Huysmans (1848–1907) – a Parisian writer much admired by Oscar Wilde – experiencing the place in the late nineteenth century.

After you've endured the shouts of programme-sellers and the solicitations of boot-blacks offering to polish your shoes, after you've passed through the ticket-barrier where, standing amid a group of seated gentlemen and assisted by a chain-wearing usher, a young man sporting a ginger moustache, a wooden leg and a red ribbon takes your ticket, the stage curtain finally comes into view, cut across the middle by the ceiling-like mass of the balcony. You can see the lower part of the cloth, and, in front of it, the two grilled eyes of the prompt-boxes and the horseshoe of an orchestra pit full of heads, an uneven and shifting field where, against the dull gleam of bald heads and the glossy pomaded hair of the men, the hats of the women stand out, their feathers and their flowers sprouting in profusion on all sides.

A great hubbub rises from the gathering crowd. A warm haze, mingled with exhalations of every kind and saturated with the acrid dust that comes from carpets and chairs when you beat them, envelops the hall. The smell of cigars and women becomes more noticeable; gas lamps, reflected from one end of the theatre to the other by mirrors, burn more dimly; it is only with difficulty that you can move about, and only with difficulty that you can make out, through the dense ranks of bodies, an acrobat on stage who is methodically devoting himself to some gymnastic exercises on the fixed bar.

For a moment, through a gap formed by two shoulders and two heads, you catch a glimpse of him, bent double, his feet braced and clamped to the bar, accelerating in a circular motion, turning furiously until he loses human form, spitting out sparks like those catherine wheels that whirl round, fizzing, in a shower of gold; then, little by little, the music which has been spinning round with him slows its spiralling pace and, little by little, the form of the acrobat reappears, his pink, gold-braided tights, shaking less energetically now, sparkle only here and there, and then, back on his feet, the man waves to the crowd with both hands.

Then, as you ascend to the upper gallery of the hall, amid women whose long trains rustle as they snake up the steps, climbing a staircase where the sight of a plaster statue holding a gas-lit torch in its hand immediately reminds you of the entrance to a brothel, the music engulfs you in your turn, feebly at first, then loudly and more distinctly at the next turn of the stairs. A blast of hot air hits you in the face and there, on the landing, you see the opposite sight to that downstairs, a completely reversed image, the curtain falling from the top of the proscenium, cut in the middle by the red ledge of the open boxes curving in half-moons round the balcony suspended a few feet beneath them.

An usherette, her pink ribbons fluttering over a white bonnet, offers you a programme which is a marvel of an art-form that is at once both spiritualist and positivist: phoney Indian carto-mancers, a lady who calls herself a palmist and a grapholo-gist, a hypnotist, clairvoyants, soothsayers who tell fortunes using coffee grounds, pianos and ocarinas for hire, job lots of maudlin music for sale, all this for the soul; advertisements for sweets, for corsets and suspenders, radical cures for intimate afflictions, a unique treatment for diseases of the mouth, all this for the body. Only one thing disconcerts: an advert for a sewing machine. It's easy to understand why there's one for a fencing school, there are a lot of stupid men about! But the 'Silent Wonder' and the 'Singer' aren't tools you ordinarily asso-ciate with the working girls who come here; unless this advert was placed here as a symbol of respectability, as an inducement to chaste labours. It is perhaps, under a different form, one of those moral tracts that the English distribute to lead creatures of vice back to virtue.

J. K. Huysmans, 'The Folies-Bergère in 1879',
from *Parisian Sketches*, translated by Brendan King

* * *

Walking around Paris, one cannot help but be conscious of the past. Many information 'shields' marking places of particular historical interest are provided by the city's administration. And there are the endless throat-constricting plaques reminding the casual passer-by that on this spot a certain human being was shot by the Nazis. If you find yourself walking around the Latin Quarter and feel like conjuring up the past, read this brief extract from the 1871 diary of Edmond de Goncourt. It was winter: the Siege of Paris (during the Franco-Prussian War) had been going on for some months ...

Friday, 6 January

The shells have begun falling in the Rue Boileau and the Rue La Fontaine. Tomorrow, no doubt, they will be falling here; and even if they do not kill me, they will destroy everything I still love in life, my house, my knick-knacks, my books.

On every doorstep, women and children stand, half frightened, half inquisitive, watching the medical orderlies going by, dressed in white smocks with red crosses on their arms, and carrying stretchers, mattresses, and pillows. [...]

Thursday, 12 January

Today I went on a tour of the districts of Paris which have been shelled. There is no panic or alarm. Everybody seems to be leading his usual life, and the café proprietors, with admirable sang-froid, are replacing the mirrors shattered by the blast of exploding shells. Only, here and there among the crowds, you notice a gentleman carrying a clock under his arm; and the streets are full of handcarts trundling a few poor sticks of furniture towards the centre of the city, often with an old man incapable of walking perched in the middle of the jumble.

The cellar ventilators are blocked with bags of earth. One shop has devised an ingenious protective screen consisting of rows of planks lined with bags of earth and reaching up to the first floor. On the steps of Saint-Sulpice, angry voices can be heard accusing the generals of treason. The paving-stones in the Place du Panthéon are being taken up. A shell has taken off the Ionic capital of one of the columns of the Law School. In the Rue Saint-Jacques there are holes in the walls and dents from which small pieces of plaster keep falling. Huge blocks of free-stone, part of the coping of the Sorbonne, have fallen in front of the old building to from a barricade. But where the shelling has left the most impressive traces is the Boulevard Saint-Michel, where all the houses on the corners of the streets running parallel to Julian's Baths have been damaged by shell splinters. On the corner of the Rue Soufflot, the whole first-floor balcony, torn away from the front, is hanging menacingly over the street.

From Passy to Auteuil, the snow-covered road is coloured pink by the glow of the fires at Saint-Cloud.

Edmond de Goncourt, *Pages from the Goncourt Journal*,
translated by Robert Baldick

* * *

One of the tourist 'must-dos' is to climb to the top of Notre-Dame – provided one is fit enough. The view from the top is still partly recognisable as the one described by Victor Hugo in Notre-Dame de Paris *(sometimes known as* The Hunchback of Notre-Dame*). Here is the view as Hugo imagines Quasimodo would have seen it in the late fifteenth century.*

When, after groping your way lengthily up the gloomy spiral staircase, which rises vertically up through the thick wall of the bell-towers, you abruptly emerged at last on to one of the two lofty platforms, flooded with air and daylight, a beautiful panorama unfolded itself simultaneously before you on every side [...]

And now, what view of the whole presented itself from the top of the towers of Notre-Dame in 1482? That is what we shall try to say.

As he reached the summit, the out-of-breath spectator was at once bedazzled by roofs, chimneys, streets, bridges, squares, spires, bell-towers. Everything struck him at once, the carved gable, the pointed roof, the turret suspended from the corner of the walls, the stone pyramid from the eleventh century, the slate obelisk from the fifteenth, the bare round tower of the castle-keep, the decorated square tower of the church, the big, the small, the massive and the ethereal. The eye was being held long at every level of this labyrinth, where there was nothing which did not have its own originality, its own reason, its own genius, its own beauty, nothing that did not belong to the art of architecture, from the smallest house, with its carved and painted front, its exposed timbers, its rounded doorway, its overhanging upper storeys, to the royal Louvre, which then had a colonnade of towers. But the principal masses visible to the eye once it had begun to adjust to the chaos of buildings, were these.

First, the City. The Île de la Cité, says Sauval, whose farrago sometimes contains these happy accidents of style: 'the Île de la Cité is made like a great ship embedded in the mud and stranded in the current towards the middle of the Seine.' [...]

The Cité was the first thing you saw then, with its stern to the east and its prow to the west. If you faced the prow, you had before you an innumerable flock of old roofs, above which swelled the broad, leaded chevet of the Sainte-Chapelle, like an elephant carrying a castle on its hindquarters. Only in this case the castle was the most daring, the most highly wrought, the finest carpentered, the most jagged spire ever to show the sky through its cone of tracery. Close at hand, in front of Notre-Dame, three streets flowed into the parvis, a handsome square of old houses. Over the south side leant the sullen, wrinkled face of the Hôtel-Dieu and its roof, which seemed to be covered in pustules and warts. Then to right, left, east and west, yet all within the narrow confines of the City, rose the belfries of its twenty-one churches, of every date, shape and size, from the low, decrepit Romanesque campanile of Saint-Denys-au-Pays, *carcer Glaucini*, to the slender spires of Saint-Pierre-aux-Bœufs and Saint-Landry.

Behind Notre-Dame, to the north, stretched the cloister, with its Gothic galleries; to the south, the semi-Romanesque palace of the bishop; to the east, the deserted tip of the Terrain. Amidst this jumble of houses the eye could still pick out, by the tall, open-work stone mitres which then crowned the topmost windows of the palace roof itself, the hôtel given by the town to Juvénal des Ursins under Charles VI; a little further off, the tarred sheds of the Marché-Palus; elsewhere again the new apse of Saint-Germain-le-Vieux, lengthened in 1458 by a bit of the Rue aux Febvres; and then, at random, a crossroads choked with people; a pillory standing at a street corner; a section of Philip-Augustus's beautiful paving, of magnificent flagstones, laid in the middle of the roadway and scored by the horses' hooves, and so inadequately replaced in the sixteenth century by the wretched cobbles known as the 'pavement of the League'; a deserted backyard with one of those diaphanous staircase turrets such as they built in the fifteenth century and of which you can still see an example in the Rue de Bourdonnais. Finally, to westward, to the right of the Sainte-Chapelle, the towers of the Palais de Justice sat grouped beside the water. The tall trees of the king's gardens, which covered the western tip of the Cité, masked the ferryman's little island. As for the river, from on top of the towers of Notre-Dame, it was scarcely visible on either side of the Cité. The Seine had vanished beneath the bridges, and the bridges beneath the houses.

And once your gaze had crossed these bridges, whose roofs, you could see, had turned green, mildewed before their time by the effluvia from the water, the first building to strike it, if it was directed to the left, towards the University, was a huge, low clump of towers, the Petit-Châtelet, whose yawning porch had swallowed the end of the Petit-Pont; then, as your eye scanned the town from east to west, from the Tournelle to the Tour de Nesle was one long ribbon of houses with sculpted timbers and

183

coloured windows, whose upper storeys overhung the roadway in an interminable zigzag of burgesses' gables, interrupted frequently by the opening of a street, and occasionally by the face or elbow of some great stone hôtel, lolling at its ease, with its courtyards and gardens, wings and *corps de logis*, amidst this populace of shabby, close-packed houses, like a great lord amidst a crowd of villeins. There were five or six such hôtels along the quay, from the Logis de Lorraine, which shared with the Bernardines the great adjoining wall of the Tournelle, to the Hôtel de Nesle, whose principal tower formed the boundary of Paris and whose pointed roofs were empowered, during three months of the year, to obtrude their black triangles on the scarlet disc of the setting sun.

This bank of the Seine, for the rest, was the less commercial of the two, the students were both noisier and more numerous than the artisans, and the only quay, properly speaking, ran from the Pont Saint-Michel to the Tour de Nesle. The remainder of the river-bank was either a bare strand, as beyond the Bernardines, or else a jumble of houses with their feet in the water, as between the two bridges. The air was full of the sound of washerwomen, shouting, talking and singing from morning till night along the bank, and pounding away at their washing as they do today. They are not the least of Paris's amusements.

Victor Hugo, *Notre-Dame of Paris*, translated by John Sturrock

❉ ❉ ❉

A little nearer to our own time, as Paris left the nine-teenth century behind and celebrated its entry into the twentieth century with the great World's Fair of 1900, it relished the new technologies that promised so much for the future. Here's a lively picture of the Fair by traveller-historian Geert Mak.

The new century was a woman, they were all in agreement on that back in 1900. Take, for example, the drawing on the cover of the piano music for the English song 'Dawn of the

Century', a 'march and two step' by one E. M. Paul. Amid golden clouds a woman balances on a winged wheel, around her float a tram, a typewriter, a telephone, a sewing machine, a camera, a harvester, a railway engine and, at the bottom of the picture, there is even a car turning the corner.

The European metropolises were feminine as well, if only in the lavish shapes of the thousands of little palaces of the bourgeoisie along the new boulevards and residential streets, with their curlicues and garlands in every 'neo' style imaginable, a ruttish profusion still found from Berlin to Barcelona.

So too the cover of the catalogue for the 1900 Paris World's Fair: a woman, of course, a rather hefty one this time, her hair blowing in the wind, a banner in her hand. Above the gate to the fairgrounds, a plaster woman six metres tall, in a wide cloak and evening dress by the couturier Paquin. At the official opening, Émile Loubet, the French president, spoke of the virtues of the new century: justice and human kindness. His minister of employment expected even more good things: gentleness and solidarity.

The fifty million visitors traipsed from one miracle to the next. There were X-ray machines with which you could look right through men and women, there was an automobile exhibition, there was equipment for wireless telegraphy, and from outside the gates one could catch the first underground line of *Le Métro*, built in less than eighteen months from Porte de Vincennes to Porte Maillot. Forty countries took part. California had dug an imitation gold mine, Egypt came with a temple and an antique tomb, Great Britain showed off all the colonies of its empire, Germany had a steam locomotive that would travel at 120 kph. France exhibited a model of Clément Ader's motorised flying machine, a gigantic bat with a thirty-metre wingspan; humans, after all, were destined to leave the earth one day.

There was a Dance Palace where a wide variety of ballets were performed, a Grand Palais full of French paintings and sculpture, and a building where the visitor could 'travel' around the entire world on a special ceiling for two francs, from the blossoming orchards of Japan by way of the Acropolis to the coasts of Spain, all depicted with extreme skill by the painter Dumoulin and his team. There was a cineorama, a variation on the panorama, where one could revel in the view from an airship or a compartment aboard the Trans-Siberian Express. The military section displayed the newest technologies in warfare: the machine gun, the torpedo, the gun turret, wireless telegraphy equipment, the personnel carrier. And completely new were the shows at the photo-cinema theatre, with newsreels accompanied by a phonograph recording. Among other things, the shaky images filmed by the Pathé Brothers showed – extra! – the Rostand family in their box at the premiere of *L'Aiglon*, and other sensations of the day: the test flight of Graf Zeppelin's first airship, the opening of a railway line through Africa, new cotton mills in Manchester, victorious Englishmen in the course of the Boer War, a speech by the Kaiser, the launching of a battle cruiser.

The map in the catalogue provides a bird's-eye view of the impressive fair grounds: from the Grand Palais, along the lanes of pavilions on both banks of the Seine, to the Eiffel Tower and the great exhibition halls on the Champs de Mars. The World's Fair was a part of the city as a whole. Or, put differently, Paris with its boulevards laid out from 1853 under the prefecture of Georges Haussmann blended seamlessly with the fair, because Paris had become a permanent exhibition in itself, the grand display window of France, the city state of the new century. And both – as the photographs in the catalogue also show – were created for the new urbanite par excellence, the boulevardier, the actor / viewer of the theatre of the street, the young people on an allowance, the noble property owner, the wealthy officer, the youthful bourgeois relieved of all financial concerns.

Geert Mak, *In Europe: travels through the twentieth century*,
translated by Sam Garrett

✻ ✻ ✻

The expectations that the new century would be governed by justice, kindness, gentleness and solidarity (see Geert Mak's piece above) seem ironic in the light of the two barbaric world wars that dominated the first half of the century alone. So much wasted human talent – like that of the French writer Irène Némirovsky who died in Auschwitz in 1942. Amazingly, the manuscript of her book depicting life during this terrible period survived to be brought to light and published 65 years later. This is how it begins.

Hot, thought the Parisians. The warm air of spring. It was night, they were at war and there was an air raid. But dawn was near and the war far away. The first to hear the hum of the siren were those who couldn't sleep – the ill and bedridden, mothers with sons at the front, women crying for the men they loved. To them it began as a long breath, like air being forced into a deep sigh. It wasn't long before its wailing filled the sky. It came from afar, from beyond the horizon, slowly, almost lazily. Those still asleep dreamed of waves breaking over pebbles, a March storm whipping the woods, a herd of cows trampling the ground with their hooves, until finally sleep was shaken off and they struggled to open their eyes, murmuring, 'Is it an air raid?'

The women, more anxious, more alert, were already up, although some of them, after closing the windows and shutters, went back to bed. The night before – Monday 3 June – bombs had fallen on Paris for the first time since the beginning of the war. Yet everyone remained calm. Even though the reports were terrible, no one believed them. No more so than if victory had been announced. 'We don't understand what's happening,' people said.

They had to dress their children by torchlight. Mothers lifted small, warm, heavy bodies into their arms: 'Come on, don't be afraid, don't cry.' An air raid. All the lights were out, but beneath the clear, golden June sky, every house, every street was visible. As for the Seine, the river seemed to absorb even the faintest glimmers of light and reflect them back a hundred times brighter, like some multifaceted mirror. Badly blacked-out windows, glistening rooftops, the metal hinges of doors all shone in the water. There were a few red lights that stayed on longer than the others, no one knew why, and the Seine drew them in, capturing them and bouncing them playfully on its waves. From above, it could be seen flowing along, as white as a river of milk. It guided the enemy planes, some people thought. Others said that couldn't be so. In truth, no one really knew anything. 'I'm staying in bed,' sleepy voices murmured, 'I'm not scared.' 'All the same, it just takes one … ' the more sensible replied.

Through the windows that ran along the service stairs in new apartment blocks, little flashes of light could be seen descending: the people living on the sixth floor were fleeing the upper storeys; they held their torches in front of them, in spite of the regulations. 'Do you think I want to fall on my face on the stairs! Are you coming, Emile?' Everyone instinctively lowered their voices as if the enemy's eyes and ears were everywhere. One after another, doors slammed shut. In the poorer neighbourhoods there was always a crowd in the Métro, or the foul-smelling shelters. The wealthy simply went to sit with the concierge, straining to hear the shells bursting and the explosions that meant bombs were falling, their bodies as tense as frightened animals in dark woods as the hunter gets closer. Though the poor were just as afraid as the rich, and valued their lives just as much, they were more sheeplike; they needed each other, needed to link arms, to groan or laugh together.

Day was breaking. A silvery blue light slid over the cobblestones, over the parapets along the quayside, over the towers of Notre-Dame. Bags of sand were piled halfway up all the important monuments, encircling Carpeaux's dancers on the façade of the Opera House, silencing the Marseillaise on the Arc de Triomphe.

Still at some distance, great guns were firing; they drew nearer, and every window shuddered in reply. In hot rooms with blacked-out windows, children were born, and their cries made the women forget the sound of sirens and war. To the dying, the barrage of gunfire seemed far away, without any meaning whatsoever, just one more element in that vague, menacing whisper that washes over those on the brink of death. Children slept peacefully, held tight against their mothers' sides, their lips making sucking noises, like little lambs. Street sellers' carts lay abandoned, full of fresh flowers.

The sun came up, fiery red, in a cloudless sky. A shell was fired, now so close to Paris that from the top of every monument birds rose into the sky. Great black birds, rarely seen at other times, stretched out their pink-tinged wings. Beautiful fat pigeons cooed; swallows wheeled; sparrows hopped peacefully in the deserted streets. Along the Seine each poplar tree held a cluster of little brown birds who sang as loudly as they could. From deep beneath the ground came the muffled noise everyone had been waiting for, a sort of three-tone fanfare. The air raid was over.

Irène Némirovsky, *Suite Française*, translated by Sandra Smith

✳ ✳ ✳

Living it up

When you're in a city as beautiful and exciting as Paris, you feel as though you're 'living it up' even when on a tight budget. In May 2003, journalist Ian Collins went to Paris for a family party – but the party fades into the background as the exhilaration of Paris (and memories of past visits) take over. Of course, that first-class Eurostar ticket with its free champagne probably helped the celebratory mood ...

To Paris for the weekend for my brother's 50th birthday, and also to visit the Louvre. What a treat. (What a trial! Will all go well?)

Time being tight, I've booked a first-class seat on Eurostar (a bargain, in my view, at £135). Bang on the button at 5.15pm the train is gliding out of Waterloo and I am glugging a glass of champagne.

Always glad to gawp into other people's windows and gardens I enjoy slurping and chomping – ah good, here comes dinner – through London suburbs. And the magically still Kent country-side seems to be held in a spell of late spring enchantment.

Then – whoosh – we're in the Channel Tunnel for 25 minutes before zooming across the vast plain of Northern France to P-A-R-I-S.

Romance spelt out in five letters.

Having spent all or part of six successive summers from the

age of 18 in the French capital, I still see arrival at the Gare du Nord as the start of a great adventure.

I've walked this city from Montmartre to Montparnasse. I've dozed in the Tuileries and Luxembourg Gardens, I've peered at the mausoleum of a Bois de Boulogne mansion where the Duchess of Windsor then lay paralysed and where Dodi Fayed later planned to install Princess Diana (before the doomed lovers entered that road tunnel beside the Seine).

At 20, I worked in a seedy hotel in Edith Piaf's rue Pigalle, where neon lights blazed red and many rooms rented by the hour. The beautiful blonde outside – who seemed to be waiting time and again for her husband to park or collect the car – turned out to be the busiest prostitute in Paris.

Now I'm heading out on the Metro and then a suburban train to St-Germain-en-Laye, where there's time for a nightcap to toast my brother, who lives here with his family, on the eve of his golden jubilee.

Next day, while others plot a party, I hit Paris.

My first goal is the Cité Metro stop beneath a flower market (mixed with cage birds on Sundays). Before the promised trip to the Louvre, I plan to tour the two islands which are the oldest part of Paris.

Sparrows mass in their hundreds outside crumbly Notre Dame as I walk toward the Ile Saint Louis, where I once spent a wonderful night in the ancient Hôtel Des Deux Îles before resuming a train journey to Barcelona.

As it starts to rain, one restaurant proves impossible to resist and I order a perfect omelette, followed by a crêpe with chestnut purée. This pit-stop pause is delayed considerably on discovery of dry Breton cider.

Although I'd always thought Paris drop-dead gorgeous, its citizens could kill you with one withering shrug or ugly comment. But here's shocking news: Parisians are now nice!

Two notices chalked on the restaurant wall appear to be rules of the house. But the one I take to mean Service Not Included actually reads Souriez c'est gratuit (Smiling is free). The second says La vie est belle profiter (Life is beautiful so make the most of it).

Boy has this brilliant city changed for the better! Bet the Louvre is even lovelier than I remember, but it's too late today – a birthday bash beckons. I'll go tomorrow.

Sunday dawns later than expected after the revelries of the night before. But I'm at Cité soon after midday, and resisting the urge to buy a pair of love birds. Can't stop. MUST get to the Louvre.

I'll just walk via my beloved Place Dauphine, where boules are played beneath the clipped horse chestnut trees.

Mon dieu! Rain again. But what's this? A fab little restaurant on my favourite square (triangle, if you must). I'll just step inside …

Wine of the month is a delicious chilled Brouilly. Great with a lentil, gammon and poached egg salad.

Outside it seems to be pouring. Oh goody. I'll just have a chocolate mousse and a glass of sauterne.

No time to do the Louvre justice now. I'll order coffee, and ogle pictures next time.

At 5.10, my Eurostar is leaving Gare du Nord, so naturally I'm lapping champagne and mentally congratulating friends who have bought a Left Bank studio since this superb service started. I've been almost two hours since lunch, I'm looking forward to dinner.

At 7pm local time, we reach Waterloo – 20 MINUTES EARLY (someone should complain).

Though lighter of pocket and heavier of stomach my spirits are soaring.

Ian Collins, 'I love Paris in the Springtime'

* * *

Paris has seen some of the most famous high-society parties in the world. Here Mary Blume describes a number that took place between the two world wars.

PARIS – It is nice to think of dressing up and smelling rose petals at a time of year when everyone is taking off his and her clothes and the pervasive perfume, if it can be called that, is Ambre Solaire.

The best dressing-up occurred in Paris between the two world wars. The occasions were costume balls of ravishing elegance. Prince Jean-Louis de Faucigny-Lucinge, who attended all of them and gave two with his late wife, Baba, a noted beauty, has described some of the better parties in his book, *Fêtes Mémorables: Bals Costumés*.

The French have been dressing up for centuries. What makes the 1920s and 1930s so particular, Lucinge says, is that it was a period when society and bohemia joined in a brief and happy mix.

"A congregation of what is called *gens du monde* and painters, poets, writers, artists – it was a mixture that created the event. Let us say Picasso would have done the décor, Valentine Hugo the costumes, Georges Auric the music, Lacretelle or Cocteau or Moran would have written a little scenario."

There would be three or four balls, for about two hundred guests, each season between April and July. Ideally they would be held outdoors, like the Faucigny-Lucinge Second Empire ball in June 1934, in the Bois de Boulogne, which ended at dawn with romantically costumed young couples rowing on the lake.

The most assiduous partygoers and party throwers were Count Etienne de Beaumont and his wife, satirized by Radiguet in *Le Bal du Comte d'Orgel* and creators of the Bal Louis XIV, the Bal de la Mer, the Bal des Tableaux Célèbres and one based on the fairy tales of Perrault to which seventeen-year-old Johnny Lucinge was invited as Prince Charming by a friend of his mother.

The boy was dazzled by the beauty of the costumes and by the appearance of his host, dressed in pink tights and tiny wings as Cupid. "He liked making appearances. Sometimes he would change his costume three or four times a night," Lucinge says.

For sheer magnificence the greatest party giver after the Beaumonts was Carlos de Bestegui, whose Venetian fete at the Palazzo Labia in 1951 was the last great ball. Lucinge's publisher insisted that he include later fetes, such as the Rothschild Proust ball and the Hélène Rochas "My Fair Lady" ball, but for Lucinge these were just collections of show biz and jet-set celebs. The party, he says, is over.

But when it was still going on, what larks! The theme would be announced several months in advance so that costumes could be made and invitations be argued over (the people one invited to costume balls were not necessarily the ones one would have dinner with). The most important part was the guest's arrival, or entrée, for which he or she might have commissioned an aubade by Poulenc or a verse by Cocteau. Sometimes guests included professional dancers in their entrées and underwent a training program to be able to keep in step. Although Elsa Maxwell once came as Napoléon III and the bearded Christian Bérard as Little Red Riding Hood, travesties were not the thing. The point was, quite simply, to look marvellous. And everyone did.

To record the evening such photographers as Horst and Man Ray would snap individuals or groups. Among the inevitable beauties at each ball were Lady (Iya) Abdy who, says Cecil Beaton, invented size, being over six feet tall, the Duchess de Gramont, Baba de Lucinge, Countess Jean de Polignac, Princess Natalie Paley and Daisy Fellowes. Chanel attracted attention among the frills of the Second Empire ball by wearing black widow's weeds and attended another party dressed as a tree.

"She adored dressing up," Lucinge says. "She was at every party and disguised herself wonderfully. It amused her, she was at the height of her glory and started going out a lot and she absolutely loved it. She took great trouble and it was always very well done because she had her own ateliers."

It was also the time when colourful revues flourished in Paris so there were many theatrical costumers near Montmartre where guests could rent costumes. Some went to great expense, while Man Ray appeared in a rayon laundry sack whose corners he had cut out for his arms and legs and carried an egg beater in one hand. The Surrealist Roland Penrose attended another ball dressed as the clock that struck at the moment Tristram Shandy was conceived.

Lucinge says he and his wife loved the planning. One of their more brilliant strokes as a young married couple was a Proust ball in 1928, only six years after the author's death. Many of Proust's friends attended and one was only narrowly persuaded not to impersonate the Master himself. The Lucinges came as the Marquis and Marquise de Saint-Loup, their costumes designed by the painter Jean Hugo whose wife, Valentine, excelled at party costumes. The party ended at 6 A.M. under the Eiffel Tower but usually they ended earlier, Lucinge says.

"People had taken such trouble to dress and prepare themselves that sometimes they weren't very comfortable and they were so excited about appearing that by two in the morning they were tired out. It never lasted terribly late."

One party where Lucinge and several other guests were extremely uncomfortable was the Bal des Matières given by the Vicomte and Vicomtesse de Noailles in 1929, at which guests were asked to wear costumes of strange materials. Charles de Noailles wore an impeccable tailcoat in oil cloth, Lucinge was a knight in paper armour designed by Valentine Hugo. "It was rather coarse packing paper. I hated it. I disliked the look of it, I disliked the look of it on myself and it was very uncomfortable. I was pleased on no account."

For the same ball, the writer Maurice Sachs pondered on whether to wear feathers or furnishing fabrics and decided instead to cover himself in pebbles, causing his dancing partners considerable discomfort. "I should have worn shells," he later wrote.

Part of the attraction of costume balls, Lucinge says, was that they gave people a chance both to play another role and to be themselves at their best. It is touching to imagine this highly sophisticated world filled for one evening with childlike excitement and a sort of innocence.

"Absolutely," Lucinge says, "and it was innocent, which is

a very strange thing because a lot of those people were more than sophisticated and yet they enjoyed themselves like children" After 1936, he says, the feeling that Europe was heading toward tragedy changed the party mood.

Even Maurice Sachs asked himself if the enjoyment of such pleasures was morally justifiable, was it right to spend such vast sums for a single night? He concluded that what he would like would be to go to the parties and not think of such things.

The parties were frivolous, of course, but frivolity is no bad thing – it has been called play at its most evolved – and it should not be confused with triviality. The costume balls celebrated the ephemeral, which is a highly sophisticated way of celebrating life.

It was a brief moment when everything was important, and nothing. "My big regret," Lucinge says today, "is that Picasso wanted to do my wife's portrait and you know how it is when one is young, one says *tant pis*, another day.

"I was young and I was lightheaded, and the painting was never done."

August 3, 1987

Mary Blume, *A French Affair: the Paris beat 1965–1999 – Essays*

* * *

A night at the Opéra Garnier is a 'must' if you really want to experience the high life in Paris – and if you can afford it. The same was true in the nineteenth century, the period of the background mystery uncovered by a twenty-first century researcher in Kate Mosse's Sepulchre. *Here's seventeen-year-old Léonie Vernier determined to enjoy a Parisian première, at all costs, and blissfully unaware of the trouble about to erupt.*

PARIS

WEDNESDAY 16TH SEPTEMBER 1891

Léonie Vernier stood on the steps of the Palais Garnier, clutching her chatelaine bag and tapping her foot impatiently.

Where is he?

Dusk cloaked the Place de l'Opéra in a silky blue light.

Léonie frowned. It was quite maddening. For almost one hour she had waited for her brother at the agreed rendezvous, beneath the impassive bronze gaze of the statues that graced the roof of the opera house. She had endured impertinent looks. She had watched the *fiacres* come and go, private carriages with their hoods up, public conveyances open to the elements, four-wheelers, gigs, all disembarking their passengers. A sea of black silk top hats and fine evening gowns from the showrooms of Maison Léoty and Charles Worth. It was an elegant first-night audience, a sophisticated crowd come to see and be seen.

But no Anatole.

Once, Léonie thought she spied him. A gentleman of her brother's bearing and proportions, tall and broad, and with the same measured step. From a distance, she even imagined his shining brown eyes and fine black moustache and raised her hand to wave. But then the man turned and she saw it was not he.

Léonie returned her gaze to the Avenue de l'Opéra. It stretched diagonally all the way down to the Palais du Louvre, a remnant of fragile monarchy when a nervous French king sought a safe and direct route to his evening's entertainment. The lanterns twinkled in the dusk, and squares of warm light spilled out through the lighted windows of the cafés and bars. The gas jets spat and spluttered.

Around her the air was filled with the sounds of a city at dusk, as day gave way to night. *Entre chien et loup*. The clink of harness and wheels on the busy streets. The song of distant birds in the trees in the Boulevard des Capucines. The raucous cries of hawkers and ostlers, the sweeter tones of the girls selling artificial flowers on the steps of the Opéra, the high-pitched shouts of the boys who, for a *sou*, would blacken and shine a gentleman's shoes.

Another omnibus passed between Léonie and the magnificent façade of the Palais Garnier on its way to the Boulevard Hauss-mann, the conductor whistling on the upper deck as he punched the tickets. An old soldier with a Tonquin medal pinned to his breast stumbled back and forth, singing an intoxicated army song. Léonie even saw a clown with a whitened face under his black domino felt cap, in a costume covered with gold spangles.

How could he leave me waiting?

The bells began to ring out for evensong, the plangent tones echoing across the cobbles. From Saint-Gervais or another church nearby?

She gave a half-shrug. Her eyes flashed with frustration, then exhilaration.

Léonie would delay no longer. If she wished to hear Monsieur Wagner's *Lohengrin*, then she must take her courage in both hands and go in alone.

Could she?

Although without an escort, by good fortune she was in possession of her own ticket.

But dare she?

She considered. It was the Paris premiere. Why should she be deprived of such an experience because of Anatole's poor timekeeping?

Inside the opera house, the glass chandeliers glittered magnificently. It was all light and elegance, an occasion not to be missed.

Léonie made her decision. She ran up the steps, through the glass doors, and joined the crowd.

The warning bell was ringing. Two minutes only until curtain up.

In a flash of petticoat and silk stockings, Léonie dashed across the marble expanse of the Grand Foyer, attracting approbation and admiration in equal measure. At the age of seventeen, Léonie was on the verge of becoming a great beauty, no longer a child, but retaining yet flashes of the girl she had been. She was fortunate to be possessed of the fashionable good features and nostalgic colouring held in high regard by Monsieur Moreau and his Pre-Raphaelite friends.

But her looks were misleading. Léonie was determined rather

than obedient, bold rather than modest, a girl of contemporary passions, not a demure medieval damsel. Indeed, Anatole teased her that while she appeared the very portrait of Rossetti's *La Damoiselle Élue*, she was in point of fact her mirror image. Her *doppelgänger*, her but not her. Of the four elements, Léonie was fire not water, earth not air.

Now, her alabaster cheeks were flushed. Thick ringlets of copper hair had come loose from her combs and tumbled down over bare shoulders. Her dazzling green eyes, framed by long auburn lashes, flashed with anger and boldness.

He gave his word that he would not be late.

Clutching her evening bag in one hand, as if it was a shield, the skirts of her green silk satin gown in the other, Léonie hurtled across the marble floors, paying no heed to the diapproving stares of matrons and widows. The faux pearls and silver beads on the fringe of her dress clipped against the marble treads of the steps as she rushed through the rose marble columns, the gilded statues and the friezes, and towards the sweeping Grand Escalier. Confined in her corset, her breath came ragged and her heart pumped like a metronome set too fast.

Still Léonie did not check her pace. Ahead, she could see the flunkeys moving to secure the doors into the Grande Salle. With a final spurt of energy, she propelled herself forward to the entrance.

'*Voilà*,' she said, thrusting her ticket at the usher. '*Mon frère va arriver …* '

He stepped aside and permitted her to pass.

After the noisy and echoing marble caverns of the Grand Foyer, the auditorium was particularly quiet. Filled with hushed murmurings, words of salutation, enquiries after health and family, all half swallowed up by the thick carpets and row upon row of red velvet seats.

The familiar flights of woodwind and brass, scales and arpeggios and fragments of the opera, increasingly loud, issued up from the orchestra pit like trails of autumn smoke.

I did it.

Léonie composed herself and smoothed her gown. A new purchase, delivered from La Samaritaine this afternoon, it was still stiff from lack of wear. She pulled her long green gloves up above her elbows, so that no more than a sliver of bare skin could be seen, then walked down through the stalls towards the stage.

Kate Mosse, *Sepulchre*

✳ ✳ ✳

The poor have always wished to emulate the rich in the way they live it up. A study of the life of the traditional Paris café sees the extreme consumption of alcohol by poorer people as a symptom of this need to identify themselves with the rich, to be seen to be 'living it up'.

Alcoholic drink, the primary item sold in cafés, should be viewed from three perspectives: as a commodity, as a symbol, and as an agent of activity – that is, in its effect on behaviour. The study of drink in nineteenth-century Paris reveals that insights on all three perspectives can be fruitfully applied. As in the case of the labor process, the Paris milieu played a vital role in shaping the drinking experience. The upper classes of this capital of fashion, luxury, and politics had traditionally viewed drink as one of the great expressions of their opulent lifestyles. The assimilation and diffusion of aristocratic eating and drinking habits brought by the Revolution, which forced the cooks of the great noble houses to open restaurants after their patrons had emigrated or been killed, made the conspicuous consumption of drink and food ever more public. It should not be surprising that lower social classes would wish to imitate such aristocratic behavior. In no other French and in few foreign cities did drink become the consummate art form throughout the class hierarchy that it did in Paris. Thus the history of drinking in Paris is as much about social aspirations as it is about social degradation and misery.

W. Scott Haine, *The World of the Paris café*

✳ ✳ ✳

The young Simone de Beauvoir, having cast aside everything she finds 'boring', describes the whirl of socializing and fun she threw herself into in The Prime of Life.

In the meanwhile I took what advantage of Paris I could. I had dropped nearly all the family connexions – with aunts, cousins, and childhood friends – that I found boring. I quite often went for lunch with my parents. As we disliked quarrels, there were few topics of conversation open to us: they knew almost nothing about my present life. My father was annoyed at my not yet having taken a job. When friends inquired for news of me, he would tell them, in disgust, that I was having my Paris honeymoon. It is true that I enjoyed myself to the best of my ability. Sometimes I had dinner at Madame Lemaire's, with Pagniez, and they would take me to the cinema afterwards. I visited La Lune Rousse with Rirette Nizan, and we finished the evening off drinking aquavit at the Vikings' Bar. I went back to the Jockey and La Jungle with my sister and Gégé; I made dates and went out with anyone – or almost anyone. Fernando had introduced me to the gatherings that used to meet in the evening at the café on the corner of the Boulevard Raspail and the Avenue Edgar Quinet, and I went there regularly. There was Robert Delaunay the artist, and his wife Sonia, who was a fabric designer; Cossio, who painted nothing but small boats; the avant-garde composer Varèse, and the Chilean poet Vincente Huidobro. Sometimes Blaise Cendrars would put in an appearance, and the moment he opened his mouth everyone uttered admiring exclamations. The evening was spent fulminating against human stupidity, the decay of society, and currently fashionable art and literature. Someone suggested hiring the Eiffel Tower and equipping it with an electric sign that read MERDE! Someone else was for sousing the world in petrol and setting it alight. I took no part in these vituperations, but I enjoyed the smoky atmosphere, the clink of glasses, and the buzz of conversation that grew louder and louder

201

as silence spread over Paris. One night when the café shut, the whole gang went off to the Sphinx, and I followed them. Because of Toulouse-Lautrec and Van Gogh I pictured brothels as highly poetical establishments, and I was not disappointed. The décor, in even flashier bad taste than the interior of Sacré-Coeur, the lighting, the half-naked girls in their flimsy harlequin tunics – all this was a great improvement on the stupid paintings and carnival booths so dear to Rimbaud's heart.

From Madrid and Budapest various artists were sent on to me by Fernando and Bandi – the latter being a Hungarian journalist in love with Stépha, whom I had known at the Bibliothèque Nationale. Night after night I showed them around Paris, while they talked to me of other great unknown cities. I also went out occasionally with a young Chez Burma salesgirl, a friend of The Tapir's, whom I found a very likable character; Sartre had christened her Madame de Listomère, after one of Balzac's heroines. We went to dance halls on the Rue de Lappe, our faces smothered in powder and lipstick, and we were a great success. My favourite partner was a young butcher's assistant. One evening, over some strawberries in brandy, he urged me to go home with him. I told him I already had a boyfriend. 'So what?' he said. 'Look, because you're fond of beef doesn't mean you can't eat a slice or two of ham occasionally, does it?' It was a great disappointment to him when I refused to countenance a change of diet.

It was seldom that I got to bed before two in the morning.

Simone de Beauvoir, *The Prime of Life*

* * *

The great Modernist writers, Proust and Joyce, though very different in their manner of writing, were universally hailed as the most important writers of their generation. Though both living in Paris, the only time they ever met was at a celebrity-packed party at the Majestic Hotel, recreated by Richard Davenport-Hines in A Night at the Majestic. *One can imagine the other guests being deeply curious about how these two very different geniuses would get on.*

It is a May evening in Paris in 1922. After several dismal, wet weeks the weather has turned warm and sunny. [...] A supper party is being held in a private dining room at the Majestic, an *hôtel de luxe* in Avenue Kléber, one of the twelve avenues named after Napoleon's generals which radiate out from the Arc de Triomphe. [...] The hosts of this supper party on 18 May 1922 are [...] a rich, cultivated and cosmopolitan English couple, Violet and Sydney Schiff. They have chosen to hold their party in the Majestic because the management of the Ritz would not permit music to be played after 12.30 at night: the Majestic, they know, vies in its splendours, comforts and cuisine with the Ritz. [...]

The 'great point in the Schiffs' favour,' according to their friend T. S. Eliot, was their capacity when entertaining 'of bringing very diverse people together and making them combine well.' [...] This Majestic evening was particularly unforgettable because Schiff had proposed to the impresario Serge Diaghilev to pay for a party at which some forty guests were invited to celebrate the first public performance of Stravinsky's burlesque ballet *Le Renard*, performed by Diaghilev's company, the Ballets Russes, and had then delegated its arrangements to the Russian. Diaghilev could muster for his productions all the greatest talents (both émigré and French) available in Paris, and had spared no pains to promote the success of the Paris Opéra evening. [...] He was equally meticulous about the sequel: the supper-party was matchless, Schiff acknowledged, precisely because Diaghilev stage-managed the proceedings as if he was directing one of his own ballets. [...] The audience at the première of *Le Renard* were jolted and provoked by some of Stravinsky's surprise effects; but the Schiffs' first-night party afterwards was even more memorable with its glittering guest-list. 'Kind Mr Schiff

203

gave a supper-party in honour of Diaghilev after the first night of some ballet or other,' recalled the art critic Clive Bell, one of the few Englishmen present at the Majestic party. 'He invited forty or fifty guests, members of the ballet and friends of the ballet, painters, writers, dress-makers and ladies of fashion; but that on which he had set his heart was to assemble at his hospitable board – in an upper room at the Majestic – the four living men he most admired: Picasso, Stravinsky, Joyce and Proust.' [...]

Long after midnight the Schiffs' guests sat down to supper. The celebratory champagne continued to be served after the last plates had been cleared by a dozen or more discreet and punctilious waiters dressed in the hotel's livery: Schiff preferred champagne above all other wines, and drank it copiously. As befitted a late-night, after-theatre supper, the food was not heavy. Schiff and the chefs of the Majestic wanted to compliment the many Russian exiles who were among the guests by providing Russian hors d'oeuvres, caviar and other light delicacies from their homeland. A light fish course, such as sole Walewska with its delicate sauce and almost imperceptible flavour of cheese, or a light meat course, such as noisettes of lamb with green beans, were requisite. But Schiff was so zealous an admirer of Proust's *À la recherche du temps perdu*, which contains so many lingering evocations of taste and smell, that he tried to turn the details and nuances of Proust's narrative into actuality in his own life. As a result Schiff shared the novelist's *penchant* for asparagus – a vegetable which Proust had beautifully and playfully described in his book – which was in season at the time of the party. Suitable choices of meat for Proustians included leg of mutton with *béarnaise* sauce (an egg and butter sauce flavoured with shallots, tarragon and chervil); *boeuf à la gelée* (spiced beef and carrots in aspic composed of best rump steak, shins of beef, calves' feet); and chicken *financière* (a tomato-based brown sauce flavoured with Madeira and garnished with seasoned meatballs, chicken kidneys, truffles, mushroom caps and green olives). Lobster *à l'américaine* (cooked with tomatoes, cognac and white wine) might be rather rich; but red mullet, or brill cooked in a white butter sauce, would surely please Proustians with a taste for fish. And for dessert there was no end of Proustian possibilities: pineapple and truffle salad; Nesselrode pudding (a creamy chestnut cake, coated with vanilla ice-cream and flavoured with kirsch); almond cake; coffee-and-pistachio ice cream; and strawberry mousse. As to the savouries, one of Proust's characters had a foible for *croque-monsieur* (cheese on toast) with a dish of creamed eggs.

About coffee time, after the food had been cleared, a shabby, confused, blundering man appeared amidst the elegantly dressed throng. 'He seemed far from well,' Clive Bell recalled. 'Certainly he was in no mood for supper. But a chair was set for him on our host's right, and there he remained speechless with his head in his hands and a glass of champagne in front of him. Between two and three o'clock appeared, to most people's surprise I imagine, a small dapper figure, not "dressed" to be sure but clad in exquisite black with white kid gloves.' The previous guest had entered the room with anxious clumsiness: the new arrival was poised, and entered with an insinuating air. The seedy drunk was James Joyce; the dapper late-comer was Marcel Proust; and this was to be their only meeting.

Richard Davenport-Hines, *A Night at the Majestic*

✻ ✻ ✻

Another Modernist, American Gertrude Stein, so central to the art scene in Paris, gives a wonderful record of life among the artists in her humorous Autobiography of Alice B. Toklas. *What better portrait of* la vie bohème *to end on than this account of a rollicking good party given for the painter known as Le Douanier Rousseau.*

Next Saturday evening at the rue de Fleurus everybody was talking about the banquet to Rousseau and then I found out that Rousseau was the painter whose picture I had seen in that first independent. It appeared that Picasso had recently found

205

in Montmartre a large portrait of a woman by Rousseau, that he had bought it and that this festivity was in honour of the purchase and the painter. It was going to be very wonderful.

Fernande told me a great deal about the menu. There was to be riz à la Valencienne, Fernande had learnt how to cook this on her last trip to Spain, and then she had ordered, but she had ordered a great deal at Felix Pontin, the chain store of groceries where they made prepared dishes. Everybody was excited. It was Guillaume Apollinaire, as I remember, who knowing Rousseau very well had induced him to promise to come and was to bring him and everybody was to write poetry and songs and it was to be very rigolo, a favourite Montmartre word meaning jokeful amusement. We were all to meet at the café at the foot of the rue Ravignan and to have an apéritif and then go up to Picasso's atelier and have dinner. I put on my new hat and we all went to Montmartre and all met at the café.

As Gertrude Stein and I came into the café there seemed to be a great many people present and in the midst was a tall thin girl who with her long thin arms extended was swaying forward and back. I did not know what she was doing, it was evidently not gymnastics, it was bewildering but she looked very enticing. What is that, I whispered to Gertrude Stein. Oh that is Marie Laurencin, I am afraid she has been taking too many preliminary apéritifs. Is she the old lady Fernande told me about who makes noises like animals and annoys Pablo. She annoys Pablo alright but she is a very young lady and she has had too much, said Gertrude Stein going in. Just then there was a violent noise at the door of the café and Fernande appeared very large, very excited and very angry. Felix Pontin, said she, has not sent the dinner. Everybody seemed overcome by these awful tidings but I, in my american way said to Fernande, come quickly, let us telephone. In those days in Paris one did not telephone and never to a provision store. But Fernande consented and off we went. Everywhere we went there was either no telephone or it was not working, finally we got one that worked but Felix Pontin was closed or closing and it was deaf to our appeals. Fernande was completely upset but finally I persuaded her to tell me what we were to have had from Felix Pontin and then in one little shop and another in Montmartre we found substitutes, Fernande finally announcing that she had made so much riz à la Valencienne that it would take the place of everything and it did. [...]

Everybody sat down and everybody began to eat rice and other things, that is as soon as Guillaume Apollinaire and Rousseau came in which they did very presently and were wildly acclaimed. How well I remember their coming, Rousseau a little small colourless frenchman with a little beard, like any number of frenchmen one saw everywhere. Guillaume Apollinaire with finely cut florid features, dark hair and a beautiful complexion. Everybody was presented and everybody sat down again. Guillaume slipped into a seat beside Marie Laurencin. At the sight of Guillaume, Marie who had become comparitively calm seated next to Gertrude Stein, broke out again in wild movements and outcries. Guillaume got her out of the door and downstairs and after a decent interval they came back Marie a little bruised but sober. By this time everybody had eaten everything and poetry began. Oh yes, before this Frédéric of the Lapin Agile and the University of Apaches had wandered in with his usual companion a donkey, was given a drink and wandered out again. Then a little later some Italian street singers hearing of the party came in. Fernande rose at the end of the table and flushed and her forefinger straight into the air said it was not that kind of a party, and they were promptly thrown out. [...]

The ceremonies began. Guillaume Apollinaire got up and made a solemn eulogy, I do not remember at all what he said but it ended up with a poem he had written and which he half chanted and in which everybody joined in the refrain. La peinture de ce Rousseau. Somebody else then, possibly Raynal, I don't remember, got up and there were toasts, and then all of a sudden André Salmon who was sitting next to my friend and solemnly discoursing of literature and travels, leaped upon the by no means solid table and poured out an extemporaneous eulogy and poem. At the end he seized a big glass and drank what was in it, then promptly went off his head, being completely drunk, and began to fight. The men all got hold of him, the statues tottered, Braque, a great big chap, got hold of a statue in either arm and stood there holding them while Gertrude Stein's brother another big chap, protected little Rousseau and his violin from harm. The others with Picasso leading because Picasso though small is very strong, dragged Salmon into the front atelier and locked him in. Everybody came back and sat down.

Thereafter the evening was peaceful. Marie Laurencin sang in a thin voice some charming old norman songs. The wife of Agero sang some charming old limousin songs, Pichot danced a wonderful religious spanish dance ending in making of himself a crucified Christ upon the floor. Guillaume Apollinaire solemnly approached myself and my friend and asked us to sing some of the native songs of the red indians. We did not either of us feel up to that to the great regret of Guillaume and all the company. Rousseau blissful and gentle played the violin and told us about the plays he had written and his memories of Mexico. It was all very peaceful and about three o'clock in the morning we all went into the atelier where Salmon had been deposited and where we had left our hats and coats to get them to go home. There on the couch lay Salmon peacefully sleeping and surrounding him, half chewed, were a box of matches, a petit bleu and my yellow fantaisie. Imagine my feelings even at three o'clock in the morning. However Salmon woke up very charming and very polite and we all went out into the street together. All of a sudden with a wild yell Salmon rushed down the hill.

Gertrude Stein and her brother, my friend and I, all in one cab, took Rousseau home.

Gertrude Stein, *The Autobiography of Alice B. Toklas*

✳ ✳ ✳

Selective Index

Acknowledgements

Oxygen Books would like to thank the many people who have supported *city-lit PARIS* with their help, advice, enthusiasm and generosity. They include (in alphabetical order): John Button, Eleanor Crabtree, Penny Daniel, Barry Davies, Daniella de Groote, Catherine Fuller, Andrew Furlow, Costa Georgiou, Chris Gribble, Mikka Haugaard, Regine Henrich, Amanda Hopkinson, Alan Jessop, Catheryn Kilgarriff, Eric and Marie Lane, Christine Legrand, Stephen May, Kate Mosse, Michael Munday, Bill Norris, Max Porter, Steve Savage, Dot and Walter Schwarz, Evelyn Simons, James Smith, Alex Stewart, Catherine Trippett, Carolyn Vassallo, Alison Wood, and Annie Woodward.

Copyright Acknowledgements

Acknowledgements

Memoirs of a Dutiful Daughter by Simone de Beauvoir, translated by James Kirkup (André Deutsch and Weidenfeld and Nicolson, 1959, Penguin Books, 1963) Copyright © Librairie Gallimard, 1958. This translation copyright © The World Publishing Company, 1959.

The Prime of Life by Simone de Beauvoir, translated by Peter Green (Penguin Books, 1965). Copyright © Librairie Gallimard, 1960. Translation copyright © The World Publishing Company.

Murder on the Ile Saint-Louis by Cara Black, published by Soho Press, 2007. Reprinted by kind permission of Soho Press.

The Bluffer's© *Guide to Paris*, published 2007 by Oval Books, London. Reprinted by kind permission of the publisher.

A French Affair: the Paris Beat 1965–1998 by Mary Blume, reprinted with the permission of The Free Press, a Division of Simon and Schuster, Inc., copyright © 1999 by Mary Blume. All rights reserved.

Sacré Cordon Bleu: what the French know about cooking by Michael Booth, published by Jonathan Cape. Reprinted by permission of The Random House Group Ltd, and Curtis Brown Group Ltd, London on behalf of Michael Booth. Copyright © Michael Booth 2008.

The Piano Shop on the Left Bank by T. E. Carhart, published by Chatto and Windus. Reprinted by permission of The Random House Group Ltd. and by kind permission of Janklow and Nesbit Associates on behalf of the author.

'A few words about Paris … ' (introduction) by Stephen Clarke. Copyright © Stephen Clarke, 2008.

A Year in the Merde by Stephen Clarke, published by Black Swan. Reprinted by permission of The Random House Group Ltd.

Les Enfants Terribles by Jean Cocteau, translated by Rosamund Lehmann, published by Harvill, Reprinted by permission of The Random House Group Ltd.

Claudine in Paris by Colette, translated by Antonia White, published by Secker and Warburg. Reprinted by kind permission of The Random House Group Ltd.

The Vagabond by Colette, translated by Enid McLeod. Reprinted by permission of The Random House Group Ltd.

'Montmartre Cemetery' by Colette, in *Parisian Tales*, translated by Helen Constantine, 2004. Reprinted by permission of Oxford University Press.

'I love Paris in the springtime' by Ian Collins. Copyright © Ian Collins, 2007.

'The Montparnasse Georama' by Gérard de Cortanze, in *Paris Portraits*. Copyright © Éditions Gallimard, 2007. Translation copyright © Amanda Hopkinson, 2008. By permission of Éditions Gallimard.

Hopscotch by Julio Cortázar, translated by Gregory Rabassa, published by Harvill. Reprinted by permission of The Random House Group Ltd.

Around the World in 80 Dates by Jennifer Cox, published by William Heinemann, 2006. Reprinted by permission of The Random House Group Ltd and David Higham Associates on behalf of the author.

'I love Paris' by Marie Darrieussecq, translated by Nicholas Royle, in *The Time Out Book of Paris Short Stories* (Penguin Books, 1999). Copyright © Marie Darrieussecq, 1999.

A Night at the Majestic: Proust and the great Modernist dinner party of 1922 by Richard Davenport-Hines, 2007. Reprinted by permission of Faber and Faber Ltd.

Gare du Nord by Abdelkader Djema . Copyright © Éditions du Seuil, 2003. Translation copyright © Heather Reyes, 2008. By permission of Éditions du Seuil.

Paris on a Plate by Stephen Downes, Murdoch Books, 2006. Copyright © Stephen Downes. Reprinted by permission of Murdoch Books.

'Un bon repas doit commencer par la faim' by Stella Duffy, in *Paris Noir: capital crime fiction*, edited by Maxim Jakubowski, 2007. Reprinted by kind permission of Profile Books.

Bouvard and Pécuchet by Gustave Flaubert, tranlsated by A.J.Krailsheimer, published by Penguin Books, 1976. Copyright © A. J. Krailsheimer, 1976. Reprinted by permission of Penguin Books.

Sentimental Education by Gustave Flaubert, translation by Robert Baldick, © 1964. Revised by Geoffrey Wall (Penguin Books, 2004). Reprinted by permission of Penguin Books.

'Cemeteries', in *Paris*, by Jean Follain. Translation copyright © Annie Woodward. By kind permission of Éditions Phébus.

Pages from the Goncourt Journal by Edmond de Goncourt, translated by Robert Baldick, published by Penguin Books. Reprinted by permission of David Higham Associates.

Paris to the Moon by Adam Gopnik, published by Vintage. Reprinted by permission of The Random House Group Ltd and the Wylie Agency, on behalf of the author. Copyright © Adam Gopnik, 2000.

Paris by Julian Green, translated by J.A.Underwood. Copyright © Champ Vallon 1983; copyright © this translation, Marion Boyars Publishers, 1991, 2001. Reprinted by kind permission of Marion Boyars Publishers.

Just Like Tomorrow by Fa za Guène, translated by Sarah Adams, published by Chatto and Windus. Reprinted by permission of The Random House Group Ltd.

Acknowledgements

A Girl in Paris by Shusha Guppy. First published by William Heinemann, 1991. Reprinted by permission of Aitken Alexander Associates.

The World of the Paris Café: Sociability among the French Working Class, 1789–1914 by W. Scott Haine, pp.1 & 88. © 1996 The Johns Hopkins University Press. Reprinted by permission of The Johns Hopkins University Press.

The Lollipop Shoes by Joanne Harris, published by Doubleday. Reprinted by permission of The Random House Group Ltd.

'Deus Ex Machina: a Short Story about Hope' by Sparkle Hayter, in *Paris Noir: capital crime fiction*, edited by Maxim Jakubowski, 2007. Reprinted by kind permission of Profile Books.

Notre-Dame of Paris by Victor Hugo, translated by John Sturrock (Penguin Books, 1978). This translation copyright © John Sturrock, 1978.

Paris: the Secret History by Andrew Hussey (Penguin Viking, 2007). Copyright © Andrew Hussey, 2007. Reprinted by permission of Penguin Books.

Parisian Sketches by J.-K. Huysmans, translated by Brendan King, published by Dedalus, 2004. Reprinted by permission of Dedalus.

Murder on the Eiffel Tower by Claude Izner, translated by Isabel Reid, published by Gallic Books, 2007. Published originally under the title *Mystère rue Saints-Pères,* copyright © 2003 by Editions 10/18, Department d'Univers Poche, Paris. Translation copyright © Gallic Books 2007.

The Père-Lachaise Mystery by Claude Izner, translated by Lorenza Garcia and Isabel Reid, published by Gallic Books, 2007. Published originally under the title *La disparue du Père-Lachaise,* copyright © 2003 by Editions 10/18, Department d'Univers Poche, Paris. Translation copyright © Gallic Books 2007.

Paris: biography of a city by Collin Jones (Allen Lane, 2004, Penguin Books, 2006). Copyright © Colin Jones, 2004. Reprinyed by permission of Penguin Books.

Sound Bites: eating on tour with Franz Ferdinand by Alex Kapranos (Penguin Books, 2006, 2007). Copyright © Alex Kapranos, 2006. Reprinted by permission of Penguin Books.

In Europe: travels through the twentieth century by Geert Mak, translated by Sam Garrett, published by Harvill Secker. Reprinted by permission of The Random House Group Ltd.

'Nightmare' by Guy de Maupassant, translated by Helen Constantine, in *Parisian Tales*, 2004. By permission of Oxford University Press.

'To the Canal Saint-Martin' by Daniel Maximin, in *Paris Portraits*. Copyright © Éditions Gallimard, 2007. Translation copyright © Amanda Hopkinson, 2008. By permission of Éditions Gallimard.

Acknowledgements

La Vie Parisienne by Janelle McCulloch. Copyright © Janelle McCulloch, Murdoch Books 2008.

Books, Baguettes and Bedbugs by Jeremy Mercer, published by Weidenfeld and Nicolson, 2005, an imprint of the Orion Publishing Group.

Europe: an intimate journey by Jan Morris, 2006. Reprinted by permission of Faber and Faber Ltd.

Sepulchre by Kate Mosse, reprinted by permission of the publisher, Orion Fiction, an imprint of the Orion Publishing Group.

Left Bank by Kate Muir, published by Review, an imprint of Headline Book Publishing. Copyright © Kate Muir, 2006. Reprinted by permission of the publisher.

Suite Française by Irène Némirovsky, translated by Sandra Smith, published by Chatto and Windus. Reprinted by permission of The Random House Group Ltd.

Down and out in Paris and London by George Orwell (Copyright © George Orwell, 1933) by permission of Bill Hamilton as the Literary Executor of the Estate of the late Sonia Brownell Orwell and Secker and Warburg Ltd. [For US rights contact Harcourt Brace.]

Life: A User's Manual by Georges Perec, translated by David Bellos (1987), published by Harvill. Reprinted by permission of The Random House Group Ltd.

Touché: why Britain and France are so different and why they do things in opposite ways by Agnès Catherine Poirier. Published by Weidenfeld and Nicolson (2006), an imprint of The Orion Publishing Group. Reprinted by permission of the publisher.

Remembrance of Things Past by Marcel Proust, translated by C.K.Scott Montcrieff and Terence Kilmartin, published by Chatto and Windus. Reprinted by permission of The Random House Group Ltd.

Zazie in the Metro by Raymond Queneau, translated by Barbara Wright, published by Bodley Head. (First published by Gallimard, 1959.) Reprinted by permission of The Random House Group Ltd, and Librairie Gallimard, France.

Zade by Heather Reyes, published by Saqi Books, 2004. Copyright © Heather Reyes 2004.

After Leaving Mr McKenzie by Jean Rhys. Copyright © Jean Rhys 1974. Reprinted by permission of Sheil Land Associates Ltd. on behalf of Jean Rhys Ltd.

Quartet by Jean Rhys. Copyright © Jean Rhys 1929. Reprinted by kind permission of Sheil Land Associates Ltd. on behalf of Jean Rhys Ltd.

217

Acknowledgements

Albertine by Jacqueline Rose, published by Chatto and Windus. Reprinted by permission of The Random House Group Ltd.

Return to Paris: a memoir with recipes by Colette Rossant. Copyright © Colette Rossant 2003. Reprinted by kind permission of Bloomsbury Publishing and by permission of Colette Rossant and the Watkins/Loomis Agency.

An Englishman in Paris by Michael Sadler. Reprinted by permission of Simon and Schuster UK Ltd., Copyright © Michael Sadler 2002.

'My love affair with Belleville' by Catherine Sanderson, copyright Guardian News and Media Ltd 2008.

The Perfect Occupation by Walter Schwarz. Copyright © Walter Schwarz. By kind permission of the author.

The Autobiography of Alice B. Toklas by Gertrude Stein, published by Penguin. Reprinted by permission of David Higham Associates.

Paris France by Gertrude Stein, published by Peter Owen, 2003. Reprinted by permission of Anova Books.

Shifts, by Adam Thorpe, published by Jonathan Cape. Reprinted by permission of The Random House Group Ltd.

Amost French: a new life in Paris by Sarah Turnbull, published by Nicholas Brealey. Reprinted by permission of the publisher.

Confessions of a Poet by Paul Verlaine, 1895; this translation © Erica King.

The Flâneur by Edmund White, published by Bloomsbury, 2001. Copyright © Edmund White 2001. Reprinted by permission of ICM Talent on behalf of the author.

'New Shoes' by John Williams, in *Paris Noir: capital crime fiction* edited by Maxim Jakubowski, 2007. Reprinted by kind permission of Profile Books.

The Twilight Years: Paris in the 1930s by William Wiser, published by Robson Books, 2001. Reprinted by permission of Anova Books.

Every effort has been made to trace and contact copyright holders before publication. If notified, the publisher will rectify any errors or omissions at the earliest opportunity.